Fighting For Our Lives:

My Battle With Cancer
to Save My Baby and Myself

by HEATHER CHOATE

Published by Mango Publishing Group, a division of Mango Media Inc.

Cover Design: Roberto Núñez

Layout & Design: Morgane Leoni

For permission requests, please contact the publisher at:

Mango Publishing Group
2850 Douglas Road, 3rd Floor
Coral Gables, FL 33134 USA

info@mango.bz

For special orders, quantity sales, course adoptions and corporate sales, please email the publisher at sales@mango.bz. For trade and wholesale sales, please contact Ingram Publisher Services at: customer.service@ingramcontent.com or +1.800.509.4887.

Library of Congress Control Number: 2017951054

Heather Choate

Fighting For Our Lives: My Battle With Cancer to Save My Baby and Myself

ISBN: (paperback) 978-1-63353-629-6 , (ebook) 978-1-63353-630-2

BISAC - REL012130 RELIGION / Christian Life / Women's Issues / Self-Help

Printed in the United States of America

CONTENTS

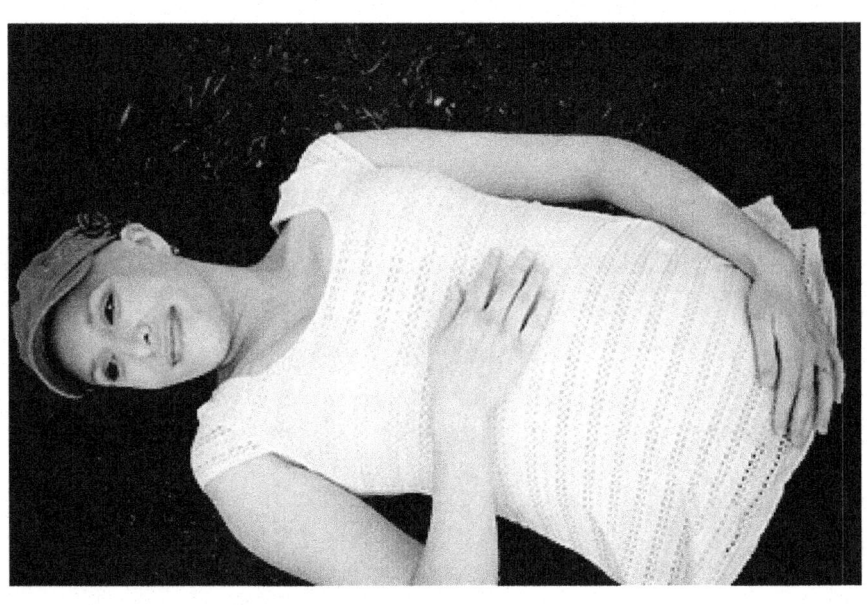

Part One
Shock

DIAGNOSIS

Wednesday, June 18, 2014

Today I found out I have cancer. The lump I noticed in my left breast was biopsied last week, and the results came in today.

I'm ten weeks pregnant. I have five beautiful children: Benjamin (7), Chance (6), Joseph (4), Morgen (3), and Naomi (1). We are so excited to have our sixth. The kids have each picked out a name for the baby. Chance loves the name "Binga." Joseph wants him to be "Sonic" (as in Sonic the Hedgehog).

Three months ago, I noticed a lump in my left breast. I was still nursing Naomi at the time, so I thought it was probably related to that, like a clogged milk duct or something. Then a month ago, after we found out we were expecting our sixth child, it really increased in size. I scheduled an appointment with my midwife for an initial pregnancy checkup. She examined the lump and said we should get an ultrasound of it, as well as an ultrasound of the baby, to determine how far along I was.

Last Friday, we went in for the ultrasounds. First, I saw our beautiful baby, healthy and well at ten weeks.

Then the sonographer looked at the lump. She took several shots, then said she wanted to send them down to the breast center to have a specialist take a look. Moments later, I was following her down long twisting halls to meet with him. He did another ultrasound there and an exam. He said we needed to do a biopsy immediately. They took three tissue samples and sent them off to the lab. He told me how unlikely it was to be cancer, or "anything serious," because I'm so young and healthy.

On Wednesday, the midwife called me. "You have breast cancer," she said. She scheduled me to meet with the surgeon in Durango the next day. "He'll want to discuss how the pregnancy hormones are going to affect the cancer."

Thursday, June 19, 2014

We went to see the surgeon specialist. He said, "There is no doubt this is cancer." He then outlined their methods of treatment. Words like "mastectomy" and "chemotherapy" buzzed in my head. None of it felt real. It still doesn't. "Now," he said, "we want to talk about how the pregnancy plays into all of this." I held my breath. Literally. I don't think I exhaled for about thirty seconds. This was the part where he would tell us the alternative options. Chemotherapy, radiation, and even hormone treatment would harm, if not kill, our baby. I was eager to hear what other answers there were to this.

"I want you to consider terminating the pregnancy."

This hit me harder than anything else I'd heard so far.

The doctor immediately went into a thorough medical explanation. "When you are pregnant, your body is flooded with progesterone, a growth hormone. It is great for growing babies, bad for tumors. Any malignant cells within your body will go on a feeding frenzy." He stopped and looked at us with us pale blue eyes. "I understand you are LDS. From what I understand, the leaders of your church support abortion in cases where the mother's health and life are in danger."

He was right. That is the church's official position.

"I encourage you to talk to your bishop about this."

Silence.

"I know it's a lot to take in."

Yes, it is.

"We recommend terminating the pregnancy and testing to see where the cancer is, how far it has spread, and what stage it is. We will do chemotherapy and then a full or partial mastectomy followed by another round of chemotherapy. In three or four years, when you show no sign of cancer, you can try for pregnancy again and have a baby. With this plan, your prognosis looks good."

I looked at Ben. His face was flat, but his eyes swam with concern.

The doctor wasn't looking for an answer now, but I already had one. I turned to him. I looked right into his eyes. "Well, I want you to know we will not be ending the pregnancy."

A frown flashed briefly across his face. "All right," he said, "but I want to be perfectly clear about this. We will not be able to treat the cancer effectively during pregnancy. The cancer will grow. It will most likely spread." He explained the hormone's effects upon the cancer cells once again, as if we hadn't heard him the first time.

"I really encourage you to talk with your bishop," he said again with great emphasis. He gave the same advice eight more times in our twenty-minute visit.

"How can we know how far the cancer has spread?" Ben asked, never letting go of my hand.

"There is no sure way of knowing unless we do the radiation testing," the doctor explained. "We will biopsy Heather's lymph nodes as soon as possible. The lymph nodes are the gateway to the rest of the body. If the cancer has spread, it will most likely pass through there, but there is also a chance it may have spread without going to the lymph nodes."

"So, as long as Heather is pregnant, we will have no way of knowing for sure."

"That is correct."

"We will do the biopsy, and then again, I really strongly suggest you go speak with your bishop."

The doctor urged the staff to get me in for the biopsy right away, but they were already booked up. We will go tomorrow. It will take two days to get the results.

So, that's what I'm facing now. At the very least, a biopsy and full mastectomy. I'm going to lose a boob. And that's so not even the important thing. I'm terrified for the life and health of my baby. I've always prided myself on being able to bear and deliver children so well.

I'm too shocked to even realize what this all means right now.... I have cancer.

I will not abort my baby. There is no alternative in my mind. I understand why some people make that decision, but it is not one I can personally live with.

I would rather die than take the life of my child.

Thursday, June 19, 2014, later the same day.

It's a gummy bear, no, it's an indistinguishable gray blob, no, it's a baby! Baby number six is on the way! Due January 9. We're very excited and feeling very blessed.

> *If you close your eyes,*
> *Does it almost feel like nothing's changed at all?*
> *And if you close your eyes,*
> *Does it almost feel like you've been here before?*
> *How am I going to be an optimist about this?*
> *How am I going to be an optimist about this…?*

That's one of my favorite songs, "Pompeii" by Bastille. It played today as I got ready in the bathroom.

It doesn't feel real. Yesterday seems like a dream. A bizarre, frightening dream, but something I can push aside, something that doesn't affect the rest of my life. Just a stupid dream.

The kids are playing. Already they're fighting. Ben's gone to work. I served breakfast, ran three miles, took a shower, put the kids in time-out, got the kids out of time-out, nursed the baby, read my scriptures, and now sit down to write. Today is the same as every other day. And yet, everything's different.

Something raw and frightening tugs at me from inside. It's a caged animal I don't want to let out. But there's something else inside too. I feel a calmness and peace I can't explain and don't deserve. *Things are going to be all right.* I'm worried the feeling will betray me as soon as I enter the hospital again and hear the doctors talking. Everything in me has tried to downplay this. Of course, I wondered and worried about what it might be, but surely it wasn't. The chances were so slim. I'm young, I eat healthy, exercise like an addict, and have five children. There's no way. There's still no way. This isn't real.

When I first found the lump, I thought it was just a clogged milk duct because I was still nursing Naomi. As her nursing slowed, I thought it was just full from carrying extra milk. But then it got bigger and hard, too hard to be just full of milk. And it didn't hurt. It never hurt. It couldn't be mastitis, because there was no sign of infection. So I started to watch it. Ben noticed too. We resolved that as soon as we got insurance, I'd go into the midwives and have them check it out. That took two months. Now I realize how precious those two months were. Is there guilt? You bet. Maybe if I had taken care of this earlier, maybe if I had acted on it before we even got pregnant, all of this could have been prevented. Probably not prevented, actually, but less complicated. But I see there is a potential blessing in this too. I might never have noticed it if I hadn't gotten pregnant. The hormones caused it to grow large enough to detect this last month.

Round and round. Circles within circles. Could-have-beens and should-haves. I'm like the spider in the middle of a web. All I can do is face what is now. It is what it is. No amount of wanting or wishing can change that.

Ben and his father will give me a priesthood blessing soon. A priesthood blessing is when a worthy, ordained priesthood holder gives a blessing by the laying on of hands for the sick and afflicted. These blessings have been a great source of peace and guidance for me in my life, and I am grateful for the opportunity to get one now, but nervous too. I guess I'm a little scared to know what Heavenly Father's will is or that I still won't know at all. But I need this baby to be safe. The baby must live. I must be able to carry the baby. Only the Lord can make that possible. Will He?

I have to feed the kids and get them ready for the day, so I really don't have more time to write. Afterwards, Ben and I will go to the hospital for the biopsy. More needles. Yay. But really, that's so the least of my worries.

Friday, June 20, 2014

I had built a cocoon of optimism and a sense of control around myself the past two days. That all shattered this afternoon.

The doctor called and told me I have cancer in my lymph nodes. It has spread past the tumor in my breast. We don't know yet if that means the cancer cells have just passed through there or if the cancer is growing within the lymph nodes themselves.

And I thought that putting deodorant on my swollen and punctured skin from the biopsy was tough enough. Looks like I'm going to need to be a lot tougher.

I'm back to my initial shock. Every step of the way I had acknowledged the possibility of the worst-case scenario, but I always believed in my heart that everything was going to be fine. *It's probably just a cyst like the one my mom had. It has to be related to nursing. Okay, now they're saying it's a tumor. It will be benign. Now, I have cancer. It's just a small tumor. It hasn't spread. It will be taken care of easily.* Every time, I believed it would be minor. Every time, it has been the worst it could possibly be. But I'm not giving up hope. I'm just feeling a little crushed by the news. It's getting more and more serious.

We met with two more doctors after talking with the first. They both told me I need to abort. My heart seems to sink further and further. One told me of a mother who did not. She delivered her baby but passed away a few weeks later. "She probably would have made it if she hadn't kept the baby," he said.

The doctor asked if we had met with our bishop. I told him we hadn't. He urged us to do so and said we would need to make our decision about treatment by Monday. My decision is made. This doesn't change anything. But that doesn't mean I'm not afraid. It doesn't mean he isn't going to think we're completely crazy.

I will never put my life before another. This is my child. I won't kill for my own health or survival. The Lord gave me this pregnancy, and His will, will be done. I would rather die than take my child's life. That may be the outcome of this. It may not. Either way, I know it is the right thing for me to do. I feel in my heart that a mother should protect her children. I feel total protectiveness of my child. Protectiveness against the cancer in my body. Protectiveness against the effects treatment can cause. Protectiveness against the very professionals and caretakers that are supposed to help us with this.

There is so much to process. I feel bombarded. So much information. Hours and hours of conversation, ideas, thoughts, hope, encouragement, fear, support and, through it all, an incredible amount of love that brings me to my knees and makes me weep tears of gratitude. It is all happening so fast, and yet so slow at the same time. It's hard to stay focused sometimes. My head spins from the whirlwind of varying emotions, the constant streams of information, and the bombardment of opinions. I feel like Nephi, in that I can't write a hundredth of what is happening and how I feel. Words are so inadequate.

Saturday, June 21, 2014

My beautiful children are playing all around me. I'm in the middle of an epic battle of Power Rangers vs. Ogres. Morgen is lying on my pillow. "I'm dead," she says. How I love them. It is shocking how precious such normal moments are to me.

"I want to talk to you about your decision," Ben's friend told him this week. "I want you to really consider terminating the pregnancy. You have your wife and five children to think about." Ben said he was pretty taken back. His friend then told him that he knew of a woman in similar circumstances. She was pregnant when she was diagnosed with breast cancer. She chose not to terminate the pregnancy. The baby lived. The mother did not.

That made this pretty real. I knew that was the risk. Hearing someone talk about someone they knew was another shock, though. I also know a woman who was diagnosed with colon cancer during her pregnancy, and she and the baby were both fine. They're healthy and well now. Miracles can occur. I have faith that they will. But I'm also not going to put blinders on and ignore the danger of our decision. We're the ones that have to live with the consequences.

I can understand where people are coming from when they tell us that. They are scared. They love me and don't want to lose me. My dad wrote me a letter reiterating what he had told me on the phone. "There is no way you should rush to any decisions until you know the full picture. But as referenced before, I have served in stakes and wards across the country and have seen countless families reach crucial decisions. Some failed. Some succeeded. Some tried and tried to get things right. But I do feel that it would be extremely wise to keep in mind the best interests of your five beautiful children, who need their mother's constant love, focus, and attention. These days will pass quickly, and suddenly they will be adults who will look back at their mother, who stood central in their lives in preparing them for life." I can tell how scared he is, and my heart goes out to him.

One of my dear extended family members expressed a similar view. I told her abortion was not something I was willing to consider. She said, "But you need to think about your five children." She is right. I do and I have. Believe me, I've thought about this more than anyone. But when I hear these things, something in my heart screams out, "I don't have five children. I have six. Five born. One coming. I must think about all of them!"

They just don't see it the way I do right now. I know they just want what is best for me. They have to trust that this is the best thing for me. I'm not afraid to die. I'm only saddened by the thought of not being there to watch my children grow, of not being with Ben as we get old together, of not being able to do all the things I've longed to do while in this mortal life. What would my children remember of me if I were gone? Have I lived my life the way I should have? Will my mistakes and shortcomings be forgiven? Will I be remembered as a good mother who did her best for her children?

Maybe in five years I'll look back and smile, knowing that I did it. And how much more I will cherish every moment because of it. But maybe not. I can't be blind to either possibility.

Everyone wants me to be positive. They want me to fight. I will. But these are my thoughts spilling out onto the page. They shouldn't be taken as me giving up. Far from it. It's just that sometimes the possibilities of this situation pound into my face. If I die, I want to be known not as the mother who foolishly didn't think of her five born children, but as a woman who loved her children so much she was willing to die for them. That is the sacrifice the Savior made for each of us. He loved us so much he laid down his own life so that we might live again. I can't hope to do what he did and feel foolish for comparing myself… But if I can be like him in any way, I must do this.

It's amazing how much you can love someone you've never met.

Everyone has a cure. I have ten emails in my inbox from well-meaning family members who love me. Everyone seems to know exactly what I should do and what will work, as if they've overcome it themselves. I can't bring myself to look at the emails right now. It's not that I don't want help or a solution. I do. It's just that it's so overwhelming. How do you sift through it all? How do you know what's real and what's just a hoax? So many people and products use "cancer cure" as a marketing ploy. I appreciate their desire to help. It's just too much. I feel completely inadequate to sift through it all and come to any sensible decision.

As for treatment, we know chemotherapy and radiation are out of the question. We have no way of knowing how far the cancer has spread or how much there is. That's where faith really has to come in. Right now, I'm willing to pursue a complete and aggressive mastectomy to remove all breast tissue and the lymph nodes. Surgery terrifies me. I've never had a major operation before. But it seems sound. I was concerned about the effect the anesthesia would have on the baby, but I feel more confident about the risks after reading about it. My mother-in-law also assuaged some of my concerns. Then, after surgery, I'll turn to alternative measures to treat any cancer that may remain. I've already cleaned up my diet. I've turned back to the Nutritarian diet of aiming to eat 90% fruits and vegetables with some legumes. Ben even had a green smoothie with me this morning. I'm still exercising and going to my counselor to get some stress management techniques and help me process all of this. We're researching cannabis oil, turmeric, and other natural treatments. There is hope. There are some amazing survival stories.

Monday, June 23, 2014

I skipped writing yesterday. I was in escape mode. Ben and I were both so exhausted. I just wanted to try and forget about all of it. Instead, I found myself curled up in a ball in Ben's arms, sobbing. He let me cry and told me it was okay. "You've been so strong," he said. "You've handled this so well. Just let it out." It was that uncontrollable, ugly cry. But it's what I needed.

Ben and I both agreed not to answer any calls or check any emails today. While I appreciate everyone's desire to help, it is too much right now. We need to focus. We have some huge decisions to make regarding treatment. We are looking at several options:

1. A complete mastectomy

2. Treatment at the University of Colorado Medical Center up in Denver. (They should have more experience with this type of case.)

3. Possible chemotherapy that is supposedly safe for the baby. (Really skeptical about that one.)

4. A naturopathic doctor in St. George who uses non-FDA approved methods to cure cancer.

These are incredibly difficult decisions to make. We have to know if they will be first, safe for the baby, and second, effective at treating the cancer. Right now, it seems like an elusive answer. I feel completely inadequate to making this decision on my own. We are pleading with the Lord to help guide us on the right path.

Yesterday, Benjamin said, "Mom, I don't want you to die." What do you say to that? We're doing our best to be open and honest with them and explain what is happening in a way they can understand without traumatizing them. That hasn't been easy. They sense the range of emotions from us, and I know they are picking up on more than we realize. We took some time yesterday to explain that what I have is serious, but that we have hope and faith. Chance stood up and said loudly, "I have faith!"

Our immediate and extended family fasted for us yesterday. I am so touched by everyone's love and sacrifice for us. Our names have been put in the temple. I got the most precious message from my niece, Adela, who I haven't seen for a couple of years. She wrote:

Hey, Aunt Heather, this is Adela. We went to Palmyra for [a] youth conference and got to see Hill Cumorah, the Joseph Smith farm and home, and the other sites as well. But we also went to the sacred grove and got to wander off on our own into the grove, so I went and found a quiet spot and I prayed for you and your baby. I was so happy I got the chance to pray for you in such a sacred and reverent place. We are fasting and praying for you, your baby, and your family. I love you, and I really want you and your baby to be ok! We all love you guys! Adela

Ben and I were both brought to tears by her words. It's amazing how much love we have felt. Yesterday, a couple we know only a little offered to help pay for part of our treatment if we need it. We were floored. The Stake President and a member of the bishopric came to visit us. They took time away from their own families to see how they could help. It is amazing how many "angels" Heavenly Father has sent us.

I really want a bit of my old routine back. That won't be fully possible, but I function best with routine. I miss writing my book. I miss doing lessons with the kids. The laundry took a week to finish, and my plants are dying from lack of water. I'm giving myself some grace with that, but those external signs are indications to me of how tumultuous our lives have become. I'm really focusing on spending some extra time with the kids. This afternoon will be another all-consuming process of trying to sift through medical information, our fears, and our decisions. All this can leave the kids feeling neglected, I'm sure. So, I'm trying to balance it all. Or at least give them time and attention when I have it.

For Family Home Evening tonight, I wanted to do something fun and freeing, and that has been on my bucket list for a while. So, we had a whipped cream fight.

It felt so good to laugh until our bellies hurt. I don't ever want to forget to live like this.

Thursday, June 26, 2014

We're driving back from Denver right now. My gum is getting stale, and we still have three and a half hours ahead of us. At least the kids aren't fighting. For now.

We met with Dr. Virginia Borges today at the Anschutz Foundation at the University of Colorado Medical Center. She's one of four doctors in the nation who specializes in young women with breast cancer and has successfully treated pregnant women. She had a very specific treatment plan for us centered on protecting the baby as much as possible while eliminating the cancer. She combines the proven methods of chemotherapy, surgery, and radiation with some cutting-edge, anti-hormone treatments all timed around the pregnancy. She said my prognosis was very hopeful.

I start chemotherapy in one week. Chemotherapy is still terrifying. More for the baby's sake than for me. But I am confident in Dr. Borges' recommendations, and we feel that it is the right thing to do. I love that she hasn't lost a baby yet. That gives me so much hope and assurance.

It's starting to hit me what all this means. Every three weeks for the next year, we'll be making a trip to Denver for treatment. I'm going to lose my hair. I'm going to face the symptoms of chemo while pregnant and parenting five children.

Friday, June 27, 2014

It feels so good to have a full day at home! No hospitals. No doctors. Just home all day with the kids. I used the time to catch up on housework, clean out my email, and take a two-hour nap while Naomi slept. I feel refreshed and recharged!

Having our treatment plan decided is a huge relief. Now I feel we can go forward with faith and determination. Ben told me this morning, "It's funny, because I never thought this was the route we would take." I hadn't thought so either.

I've been listening to doctors and nutritionists talk about how cancer can be overcome and prevented with diet my whole life. I was a firm believer, and I still am. I turned to the raw foods lifestyle two years ago to give me and the babies dependent upon me the best nutrition possible. But I still got sick. I think prevention is important. We do need to change our eating habits and lifestyles as Americans. But I think the "experts" need to be careful about their claims. I have lived an exceptionally healthy lifestyle this past year. I ran a half marathon just a couple of months ago. But I still got cancer. Saying that all disease is based upon environment, nutrition, and lifestyle can cause people to feel unnecessary levels of anger, guilt, and frustration. The diet is sound. It will help me recover, but I've come to the conclusion that it alone is not enough to help me overcome this. And that's okay.

I know the Lord has led us to the right treatment plan. Both Ben and I could feel the Spirit as we figured it out. All the confusion and worry seemed to fade away. Things became clear and focused. I've prayed about it several times since. Again, I feel like it is the right course for us. My sister Jasmine spoke to a very well-known doctor in L.A. whose patients come from all over the country. He told her to give me a piece of advice. "Tell her that the natural methods are important for strengthening and supporting the body, but they are usually not enough." That statement made it very clear for me and resonated with my soul. I really wanted to use an all-natural approach to cure this cancer but found many were just as dangerous (if not more so) for the baby or were simply not effective enough. I think we have chosen a treatment that will be effective on the cancer *and* safe for my child. We pleaded with the Lord to help guide us. I know He has answered our prayers. As terrified as I am, I have faith this is the best course for us.

All I have to say is this is a beautiful day and this is a wonderful life.

Saturday, June 28, 2014

It's funny how the business side of me comes out as we discuss and weigh
our treatment options and plan, but then the emotional side creeps up and
surprises me. I thought I had my head wrapped around this thing. Then last
night I had a dream where I saw each of my children standing over my grave.
It was exceptionally real. I was watching them from across the casket, but they
couldn't see me. I wanted so badly to hold each one of them. I felt no pain, but
my heart broke in a way that could never be mended. I saw Ben gather all the
kids around and say, "Okay, kids. Now it's time to say goodbye to Mommy."

"What do I say?" Joseph asked, not looking at him, turning his foot in
the grass.

Through red, teary eyes Ben said, "Just tell her that you love her. You can give
her a flower."

Benjamin was crying. He looked a little bit older, maybe nine years old. He put
a flower on my grave and said, "You were the best mom ever. Now I'll never
have a mom again." He broke into sobs. Ben held him and let him cry.

Chance stepped up, looking really hard, as though trying to be brave. He said,
"I have faith that if I choose the right, I'll see you again." He threw a white
flower on the casket.

My mother-in-law, Ginger, prompted Joseph to step forward. He buried his
face in her skirt. "Just tell her bye-bye, baby," she told him gently and quietly
enough so only he and I could hear her.

"Goodbye, mom," he said in his low, quiet voice.

Morgen twirled in circles a little way off. She wore a pale yellow dress, her favorite color. She'd gathered a large assortment of flowers and was singing softly to herself. Ben called her over, "Morgen, come say goodbye to Mommy."

She shook her head but came. Ben knelt beside her as she squirmed. "Do you want to give Mommy a flower?" he asked. Again she shook her head, frowning. She clutched her bouquet close to her chest.

"These are my flowers."

"Don't you want to give one to Mom?"

"No."

He hugged her. "Okay. That's all right."

He turned back to the grave.

"I do! I do!" she called out loudly.

"Okay, that would make mom happy."

Morgen took her time picking one out. Finally, she pulled out a pink and white lily, one of my favorites. "Here," she said, handing it to Ben.

He set it on the casket.

"Do you want to give mommy a kiss?"

She nodded. Together, they knelt and blew me a kiss.

My mom came next, holding Naomi. She was walking and talking, but still so small. "Wave bye-bye," my mom said. She waved her chubby little arm in imitation.

A short way away, my grandmother, Susi, held a beautiful baby in a white blanket. The baby wasn't even a year old. But it was whole and wonderful. I brushed its cheek and kissed its forehead. but couldn't even feel its skin.

I don't want to leave them, not now and not ever. They are everything to me. I love them more than they will ever know. Tears are streaming down my face as I write this. I didn't want to put this in my journal, but I have to be true to what I'm going through. It's not all hope and optimism. It's not all doom and gloom. It's a bewildering, awful, and yet beautiful mixture of both.

Two people have told me in the past several days that they admire how strong I am. I don't feel strong. I feel overwhelmed, exhausted, scared, and hopeful at different times. I show a confident face. I cry. I try not to pretend to be anything other than who I am. Am I strong? I don't know. I'm not sure what strength in this situation means. But under all the fear, anger, faith, and frustration, there is an unshakable conviction within me that I am doing the right thing. This isn't about me. This is about my baby. The only thing that matters is that she lives. I will do everything I can to protect her. These aren't just words. Sometimes reading them on the flat page can make them so easy to gloss over. "Oh, that's a nice sentiment." That's not the case here. These are the convictions of my soul. They are written into my heart and are stronger than iron and go deeper than a chisel in granite. I will seal them with my actions, with my life. I'm not afraid of pain. I'm not afraid of death. I'm not afraid of suffering. I will do it all, so she can live.

Monday, June 30, 2014

"It's not about what you do, it's about who you become."
–Robin Sharma

I listened to one of my favorite leaders, Robin Sharma, this morning as I ran on the treadmill. He shared the idea of top performers who set mastery goals vs. ego goals. Ego goals are doing things to look better in the eyes of others. Masters set mastery goals. He says, "It's not about, wow, look world, how great I am. It's not about fame, fortune, and applause. It's about mastery. These goals are all about you expressing more of your potential. You getting better at your craft. You developing more acumen, more focus, more persistence, more grit."

This experience has caused my goals, the things most important to me, the things I'm willing to get up in the morning and fight for, to change. I'll admit I was very ego-driven these past few years and probably for most of my adolescent and adult life. I yearned for the spotlight. I thrived on the theatrical stage in high school and college. I wanted people to recognize my talent, my creativity. Yes, I wrote because I love writing and creating. I have a wonderful imagination that I delight in letting loose. But I also used that craft to propel myself forward in "worldly success." I wanted others to recognize me. I wanted to be valued. I wanted to feel accepted.

And that isn't necessarily a bad thing, but now I realize what a shallow thing it is. It is good for us to want success. It is good to grow and stretch ourselves. It is good to cultivate our talents and share them with others. But now I understand it's not so much about what I do, it's about who I am and who I am becoming.

Time is short.

We always hear this, but how often does it really sink in?

What if today were my very last day? What if this is my last year? To me, these aren't just philosophical ponderings anymore. They are reality. This could be my last day. This could be my last year. Have I done what I was supposed to do? Have I become who I wanted to be? What regrets do I have? What choices do I have?

What will I make of my life, no matter how long or short it is? Do we recognize what a precious gift each day is?

I want to set some mastery goals for this experience. I want to create a focused vision that includes what I want to achieve with this, who I want to be, and whose lives I want to make better because of it.

Robin further says, "Goals that are designed to please the herd and fit into society don't have the same power as goals based on intrinsic motivation, which is all about becoming more masterful, expressing more potential, and even changing the world."

Will I change the world? Probably not. But maybe I can change someone's life. Maybe I can give hope to someone who is struggling. Maybe my story will give clarity to someone facing difficult choices.

I can sit behind my computer, hide in my house, and wallow in self-pity, or I can allow myself the chance to affect someone else's life for the better. There has to be a reason this has happened. Maybe this is it.

I'm going to think about this a little more today. What is it I want to take away from this? How can I use this to help others? Who do I want to be on my final day?

Why do we put off becoming who we really want to be? Why do we wait to live the kind of life we want to live, hoping someday it will fall into our lap?

I have a lot of regrets. After my dream of seeing each of my children say goodbye to me over my grave, I woke up with a horrible feeling of guilt in my chest. Guilt for the times I have acted out in anger against my children. Guilt for losing my temper.

How long have I wanted to change? How long have I said, "I will never yell again?" I have made improvements over the years. I have learned to temper myself and think more often before I react. But I am far from perfect. I can do so much better. Whether my last day is sooner or later, I want to know on that day that I am the mother I've always wanted to be. I love this quote:

"Live so that when your children think of fairness, caring, and integrity, they think of you."
–H. Jackson Brown, Jr.

That is the legacy I want to leave. I want my children to know, above all, that their mother loved them more than anything. That is a huge focus for me. Nothing else is as important. Health comes and goes. Money comes and goes. We are born and we die. All that remains with us is our character and the influence we have had upon others.

So, that's number one for me in my mastery goals:

I am master of my emotions and actions. I temper anger. I subdue frustration. I speak and act with the love that burns in my heart. I am only as strong as I am calm.

Begin with the end in mind.
−Stephen Covey

Those words have stuck with me. If you want to change who you are, know who it is you want to be. Visualize exactly how you want to think, act, and be. See the end now.

Here's number two of my mastery goals:

In one year's time, my son is whole and healthy. I can feel him in my arms. My body is cancer-free and whole. I have a long and healthy life ahead of me.

I wrote this in the present tense because I heard neuroscience has proved the subconscious only understands present-tense language. It may sound silly, but I think it is powerful. To repeat these mastery goals and do these visualizations often is important.

Friday, July 4, 2014

I love this day of celebration of our nation's independence! We have so many things to be grateful for. I am thankful for the multitude of opportunities I have.

I was supposed to do the first chemo treatment yesterday. Ben and I both felt like we should listen to the counsel given in the blessing to wait until we talk to Dr. Borges before proceeding. The problem is, she is out of the country until

Tuesday, and no one has been able to get ahold of her. It was a huge test of our faith. It was one of the hardest decisions we've ever made. Ben said this morning, "It was one of the worst days of our lives." Logic says we should have done the treatment yesterday. The doctors were encouraging it. My mom was all right with taking care of the kids, and the timing was perfect. I don't know why the Lord wants us to wait to talk to Dr. Borges, but I do know that as soon as we made that choice, we both felt peace. Maybe the baby just needs another week. A week won't make that big of a difference to me, but at this point, it could make a huge difference for her.

It was hard to come home to my mother's worry and concern. She told us about the young mother that led us to Dr. Borges. Her treatment was delayed, the cancer spread, and she died a few months after having her baby. I've heard several other stories as well. But I know we made the right decision. If we don't do this the Lord's way, how can we expect to receive His blessings? These choices are impossible to make on our own, but with the Lord, all things are possible.

Sunday, July 6, 2014

Some wisdom from Kermit the Frog. And so true. Dozens of people are fasting for me and the baby again today. Many of them I don't know. That's pretty amazing. And humbling.

I've been a pretty private person. It's not that I haven't wanted other people to help me, but I've felt that because I was the one who chose to have five children, when other people did not, it should be my responsibility to take care of them. It's a lot to ask of people. My friends have been absolutely amazing during this experience. They have opened my eyes and heart to the generosity of others. I'm learning that it's okay to let go of control and that others can be trusted to be there. They want to help. People have dropped everything to watch the children for hours while Ben and I were at the hospital. My Mom spent five days with us after her long trip to LA. It was so good to have her there so soon after we found out. There's nothing like a mother's hugs, though I can't imagine how scared she must have been. Ben's parents drove up the day after we found out. Sweet women have brought me dinner, flowers, and letters. They made freezer meals, wrote letters, tied me a fleece blanket, and brought the kids treats. Families in Denver have opened their homes to us. That kind of stuff just blows me away and brings tears to my eyes. We humans really are amazing. It's incredible how people come together to help in times of need. I feel so grateful and so blessed. I know the Lord has answered our prayers through others.

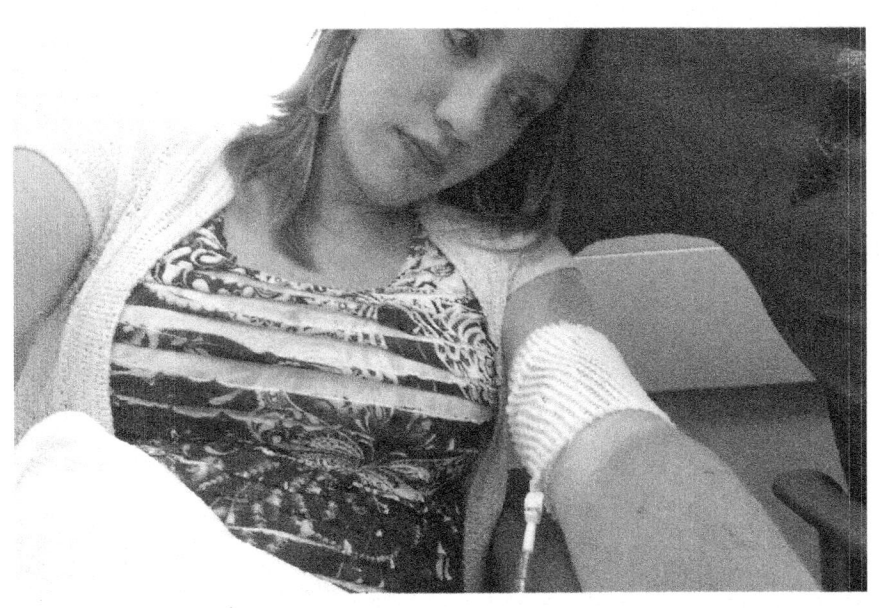

Part Two
Chemo

TREATMENT

Tuesday, July 08, 2014

Safe Shores

Poison falls around me like red rain,
But the cloud is inside me,
Swirling through my heart,
My lungs, my veins.
Red in my sweat, my tears,
Seeping out of my cells
Like the silt of the Nile river,
Dissolving health and disease
In its destruction.
I feel it pounding through me,
A flood I cannot escape.
And I'm not alone.
No, not alone.
If I were the only casualty,
How my heart would rejoice,
But I am not alone.
There is another victim here,
One innocent and small and pure.
No illness plagues her body,
But the poison floods her as well.
How do I protect her?
There is no umbrella to stave off this rain,
No shelter,
No warm embrace,
No way to soothe her cries,

Or ears to hear her pain.
Red rain fills her veins,
Combating every growth,
A sword over an infant's head.
What mother wouldn't step before the blade?
But the blade is inside me.
I cannot fight it,
Cannot shield her from it.
Helpless before the torrent of toxicity,
The biohazard we both have become,
I lie here completely helpless to save you.
But there is one who is mighty, who can save.
One who can go beyond the flesh
And raise from the grave.
It is in Him that I must trust,
Like Miriam sending Moses forth on the water,
Unsure and afraid,
But clinging to a desperate hope,
A basket of faith,
To save a life that the poison longs to take.
With her, I sing a pleading song,
The rawest begging of my heart,
Bear her safely
Across red waters.
She is helpless, and so am I,
But you alone
Can bring her to safe shores.

I often feel I am walking this path alone. What mother has to face these fears? These choices? How can I be willing to do something that could harm and even kill my child? The doctors keep telling me the risks are small, the percentages low. I want to ask them, "Would you give poison to your child, even if there were only a 5% chance it would kill him? Would you do it if the chance was 1%?" I would do anything to protect my children. This unborn baby is my child. Can any heart understand that?

When I feel alone is when I feel the Savior the most. He walked a path no human has ever tread. I'm beginning to understand Him better. He took a lonely road, and He did it for us because He loves us. He was utterly and completely alone. I am not. He is there. He knows me. He bore our sins, our sorrows, and every infirmity of the flesh so that He would know how to succor us. I feel His arms around me. I have felt closer to Him in this than I ever have before. Part of it is out of my desperation, but mostly it is His mercy.

I am not strong. But He is. I am not all-knowing. But He is. That is why I must rely on Him. I must follow the promptings of His spirit to guide me in this. Does He want to call me home? Does He want me to live? Will He protect my baby? Will we both live and be healthy? Or will the road be long and hard? Will it be shorter than we now realize? These are the things I don't know. Am I willing to accept His will no matter what it is? Will I trust Him even if that means He takes me from my husband and children? Will I trust Him even if it means I must go through pain, fear, and sorrow? Will I trust His will if He saves me but takes my child? That one is the hardest for me to accept. I don't know if I would have the strength to endure that. But what if He requires that of me? Will I still have faith? Will I submit to His will? Who would I be if the Lord took everything away from me, my health, every person I love, every possession I have, as He did with Job? Would I remain faithful still? Am I strong enough for that?

I don't know the answers to these questions that tumble around inside me like boughs in the wind. But I do know that the Lord is with me now, and that is enough. I have to have faith that through the Lord, I can do all things. Now and throughout my life, I must stay close to Him. I must listen to the quiet promptings of the Spirit. Even if I am well and whole again, I must never forget whose hands my life is really in. I must rely on Him as fully then as I do now. Only He will safely navigate me through this life. Only He will bring me safely home again. When my life is through, I want the Lord to say, "Well done, thou good and faithful servant. Thou hast been faithful over a few things, I will make thee ruler over many things: enter thou into the joy of the Lord." (Matthew 25:23).

Friday, July 11, 2014

Chemo is coursing through my veins right now. We went up to Denver early in the morning on Wednesday and met with Dr. Borges at one. She answered the question we needed to ask her, and the Spirit gave us 100% assurance that doing chemo and surgery while pregnant was the right course for us. No time was wasted after that. They whisked us down to the surgery section and had a PICC line placed in my left arm with a catheter that went all the way up my shoulder into the main vein just above my heart. We then went to the cancer center infusion treatment area. They hooked the PICC line up to the IV fluids and started with pre-meds and saline solution first. I told Ben, "It feels like we're at the top of the rollercoaster. We've heard that last "click," and now we're just waiting to fall."

Next, a nurse came in with three large syringes of red liquid, the Adriamycin. Tears streamed down my face as I watched that red liquid travel through the IV line and into my body. "This is it. No stopping the train now." I prayed a hundred times that day, "Please keep the baby safe."

Though I knew we were doing the right thing, I was still terrified. If it was just me going through this, I could take it. But knowing the poison was getting through to my baby to some degree was the most horrible feeling I've ever had as a parent. My faith felt weak – not that I doubted, I just couldn't stop pleading with Him. He'd already given me the answer, so I suppose I shouldn't have had to ask Him so many times. I should have just trusted in what He already told me. But watching that red liquid pour into me seemed to overpower almost everything else. I may not be able to stop praying like that until the baby is in my arms.

I began to feel the effects within an hour after the infusion finished. I told Ben, "It feels like I'm at the bottom of a well." I got a headache and felt incredibly tired and a little weak. We drove to Colorado Springs and picked up the children from Ben's brother's house. They were happy to see us.

Chance asked, "Did you take the bald medicine?"

"Yes, I did."

He frowned, looking at my head. "Then why do you still have hair?"

"It will take a few weeks for it to fall out."

His eyes got really big. "I think I saw some fall out right now!" Then he ran off to go play fire trucks with his cousins.

We stayed the night at Ben's other brother's house, but none of us slept well. The children were hot and uncomfortable. I woke up several times feeling like I would vomit. I had to use the restroom a lot, too, and I am terrified of developing cystitis, where basically the chemo eats away at the bladder, causing inflammation. The next day, Ben let me sleep in while he took care of our early risers. (Naomi got up at five!) And then we went over to visit his parents for a few hours.

I was out of it and still really tired. My headache hadn't gone away. Ben's parents understood, and it was good to visit with them. Ginger, my mother-in-law, understands my feelings towards my unborn child and my willingness to do anything to protect her. She comforted and reassured me.

Then we made the seven-hour drive back to Bayfield. The children were tired. I slept several hours. Ben and I both agreed that we would not bring them with us in the future. It was exhausting both for us and for them. I hate leaving them, but I think that will be the best option going forward. They can stay more on their normal schedule, and Ben and I can get the rest we need and give more focus to my treatment and recovery.

I asked two good friends to come and watch the kids for me today, and I'm glad I did. I'm super grateful for them. I napped until noon and will probably lie down again in a little while. The chemo has hit me harder than I thought. It feels like someone has sedated me and I can't come out of the fog. Luckily, I haven't vomited, but my appetite hasn't been great either. I just read the following from registered dietician Patrick Quillin: "Malnutrition kills more than 40% of cancer patients." So I forced myself to eat some eggs and a fruit smoothie. I need to make sure the baby is getting good nutrition as well, in order to give him the best chance to fight this.

I've felt a huge outpouring of love and support. I know it has helped us, and I'm very grateful. It's strange, though. Even with my husband and loved ones right here, I can still feel very much alone. At the crowded gas station yesterday, dozens of people bustled in and out, getting fuel, using the restroom, buying drinks and snacks. But I was the only one with chemo coursing through me. I was the only one fighting for two people's survival.

It's a quiet, lonely battle.

But I know He's there.

Monday, July 14, 2014

Adriamycin (Also known as "red death")

Day five since chemo. It hits me in waves. Sometimes I feel pretty good. Then, wham! It hits me, and it's as though someone sedated me. I feel drugged. Exhausted. Unable to keep my eyes open. I've slept four to six hours every day since receiving treatment. That's in addition to sleeping eight to nine at night. I couldn't do this without the amazing amount of help I've received from good friends, as well as Ben.

The nurse administering the chemo told us the heart has a limit to the amount of Adriamycin it can handle across a lifetime. He told us this as he was pushing the red liquid into my IV.

"How much can it withstand?" Ben asked.

"Nine doses."

"Nine?"

"That's right. This is number one for you."

If I had nine more after that one, I'd be dead. From heart failure. End of story. I'm scheduled to receive four doses during pregnancy. I'm not sure how many more after the baby is born.

"That's why we did the echocardiogram to monitor your heart," the nurse explained. "We want to be very certain of the chemo's effects on it."

Chemo is an amazing science. Give too much, and it will eventually kill the patient. Give just the right amount, and it will target the cancer, killing it and all the other rapidly dividing cells in the body first.

I've just received the first dose of a drug powerful enough to stop my heart once the limit of nine doses is reached.

So what did I do today? I ran. I needed to feel my heart pounding, healthy and strong despite the slight pull of the drugs I can feel on it. Three months ago I ran a half marathon. I never worried about the strength of my heart then. But now, look what I've done to it.

My friend picked the kids up. They would be gone all day, so I decided to take an hour and run to the end of our drive and up a mountain trail through the forest to a nice overlook. I had to stop and walk up the hills more than I wanted to. As I made my way up, the words of this poem played around in my head:

Have Me

I run because I need to know this heart is mine.
Kill the cancer.
You can't have me.
But the drugs are there behind each breath,
Pounding in my temples,
Leaving a briny taste in my mouth
That mixes with the salt of my sweat.
There is life around me.
Beauty, stillness and quiet,
A sacred grove,
Nature's temple.
Sunlight hits my cheek,
Wind blows my hair.
Yes, I have one week of hair-life left.
Birds call, and crickets chirp.
The air is humid from the storm the night before.
The forest smells sweet,
Of pine and damp earth and leaves.
A bull snake bathes on the road.
He is as rigid as a rod as I pass

As if I am something to fear.
My heart pounds,
I feel the impact in my hips,
My ankles and knees.
These shoes have gone many miles with me,
But none like this.
The fog over my mind doesn't lift,
But it doesn't consume me.
Underneath it I feel a sense
That despite it all,
I'm still me.
I reach the overlook.
A green valley bathed in morning light
Stretches like a sea before me.
But suddenly, I can't see it.
My eyes are swimming with tears.
I was thinking of Joseph,
My four-year-old son, so full of joy.
Will I know him years from now?
Will I watch him grow?
Will he know who I am?
Have I done enough to show him truth in lies?
Will he cling to the Savior as I do now?
Will I see him struggle and succeed?
The blue and cream clouds above
Remind me of the place
I do not want to watch from.
I chastise myself for the unexpected thoughts.
Don't think like that.
Stay focused on being well.
"90% of the battle is staying positive."
"I'm not going to die."
But what if He does call me home?
What if, after it all,

That is what happens?
Am I prepared?
No.
I push the traitor tears from my face.
My hand rests on the slight bulge of my abdomen,
The life growing within.
Just then, in the distance,
An eagle cries.
The sound of freedom,
How can it not make a heart rise?
Liberation, beauty and choice
All echo within the sound.
Freedom.
I want freedom.
But the prison is inside me.
One hand on my heart,
One hand on my stomach,
Inside there is death,
But inside, there is also life.
I run because I need to know this life is mine,
Even if it is just a moment.
Kill the cancer.
You can't have me.

Tuesday, July 15, 2014

I'm still suffering from the effects of our first chemo treatment, but so far, the baby seems safe.

We will do four chemo treatments total while I'm pregnant, one every three weeks for a total of 12 weeks. That will bring me close to the end of the second trimester, when we will do a full mastectomy.

Then we will give the treatment a break in the third trimester, to bring my and the baby's blood cell counts up to prepare for delivery. I should be able to deliver normally, though there is a greater chance of earlier delivery and low birth weight.

Four or five weeks after the baby is born, we'll hit the cancer hard with chemo, radiation, and anti-hormone therapy.

I'm continuing to aim for optimal nutrition as well (you can learn about my clean eating lifestyle on my blog) to help support my body during the treatment and give my baby the best start possible.

Wednesday, July 16, 2014

The baby is doing well. We heard his heartbeat strong and fast at the midwife's. Hearing that sound, Ben and I shared a look that I will never forget. It was the best news I've had since this whole thing began.

Knowing how the chemo has affected me this past week, I keep wondering how much is getting to her and how it is affecting her. But her heartbeat is strong. She is doing all right. And I am so grateful.

This past week has been a haze of bouts of extreme fatigue, nausea, and headaches. It's hard to come out of the fog or feel really "present." I've slept several hours every day. I miss being myself around the children. But it's supposed to get better from here. Until two weeks from now, when they do it again. It makes me treasure the moments that I do feel good and recognize what a gift each day is.

Friday, July 18, 2014

I have about seven days of hair-life left. Ha ha. Who knew there would ever be an expiration date on my hair? We're going to have a big head-shaving celebration to commemorate the change. The kids seem pretty excited and nervous about it. I bet I'll be the only bald, pregnant, boob-less woman in the state of Colorado. It's a pretty big achievement. At least it gives us something to laugh about!

Sunday, July 20, 2014

Frustration has been building in me like a big gray storm. Here we are at day eleven, and I'm still feeling sick several hours of each day. It's not all day, so it is getting better, but I had an expectation that I'd pretty much be feeling like my old self by now. Not so. It makes me mad. So this is me venting. I'm tired of not feeling like myself. I'm tired of not being mom, not being wife like I'm used to being. I'm the one who fixes things. I'm the one who makes things better. Now, I can't even fix myself. I want it all to go away. I want to feel normal again. I wish I could make it so. I don't like being a burden and strain on my family, especially Ben and all the people helping us out.

I'm feeling overwhelmed, because this is the first treatment of so many more to come. We have to go back in a week and a half. Then it starts all over again. How am I going to handle this with a newborn? How am I going to be the mom to him that I want to be? I've been doing so well, taking this a day at a time, and now I'm thinking too much about the future and all that this treatment means for the next year. It's overwhelming me. That's been the source of most of my anxiety in the past, worrying too much about the future and letting it all build up inside me. This is the first time since my diagnosis that I'm really feeling all these unknowns weighing on me. I know I need to put my focus on the present, but I'm not sure how to do that right now. I am sick and frustrated and not feeling too good about this right now.

Tuesday, July 22, 2014

I decided I'm going to abuse my hair this last week while I have it. Washing it every day, blow dryers, curlers. What would you do if you knew your hair would only last a week?

Thursday, July 24, 2014

I'm sitting on the edge of my bed right now, holding a fistful of my hair, thinking, "I'm not afraid to be bald. I'm not afraid to be bald." But every time I run my fingers though my hair, more strands fall out in mean clumps, and it feels like something is being taken away from me. My femininity perhaps? I'm more than my hair. I know that. It will grow back. I know that too. So why am I trembling and fighting back tears while I hold this hair?

Hair is nothing, really. Just dead cells. But that's me trying to be rational about this. It isn't working. I knew this would happen. I thought I was prepared. I honestly didn't think it would be this traumatic. Words like "ugly" and "freak" are going through my mind. My self-worth isn't based on hair, right?

Now that it's started, there's no going back. I won't be the same next week as I was this week. What am I going to do? Cover it up with a wig? That seems so fake. Like I'm pretending to be something I'm not. I'll be bald. That's the truth. Anything else feels so false. But will I be able to face a mirror, or go out in public, or come to bed without hair? Even fake hair?

The hair comes off my head like water slowly dripping from branches. It leaves me with yet another opportunity to ask myself how I'm going to handle this.

Monday, July 28, 2014

Three days left of feeling like me. I'm feeling almost as well as I did before the chemo started. The fatigue and nausea have passed, and I've been dealing with the more annoying side effects, like my hair falling out, the stomach cramps, and the mouth sores that hurt so bad I can barely talk or eat. But those things are livable and not debilitating, and I'm grateful to have my energy and focus back.

Ben's parents are coming tomorrow, and they'll be here a week to help me get through this next round. I'm so glad. I really need Ginger's soothing hugs and understanding. She's always there when I need her, and she never pushes Ben or me. She simply gives the help we need. I am grateful for that. It's not easy for them to get away and travel so far. I'm grateful for their sacrifices and those of the rest of the family that make it happen. I've learned how important it is to ask for help. I need and accept it.

The Lord has answered our prayers through many people. He has also answered them through our new companion, Sadie. That may seem silly, but I know He knew exactly the dog we needed at this time to bless and enrich our lives. We've wanted another dog to fill the place that Mohan, our pit bull/chocolate lab mix, left. Not just any dog would do. We needed one that would fit our lifestyle: responsive, house-trained, well-behaved, with a desire to please.

Sadie is that and so much more. She is only a year old, but she is calm inside, doesn't make messes or destroy anything, and is fun and playful outside. She fetches balls and leaves them. Even for Morgen! The kids adore her. They're playing in the kiddie pool with her right now. She sleeps on Benjamin's bed.

Her temperament is so loving and eager to please. Ben is already teaching her tricks and to stay lying down in the living room during meal times. She is the perfect fit for us. I really believe that the Lord led us to her, because she is just what we need right now. She's my "therapy dog" because she brightens my mood and brings so much joy to our family. So yeah, the Lord sent another angel to us, this time, a canine version.

We just shaved my head. When three strands of hair fell into my food at dinner tonight, I decided enough is enough. Though I didn't look like I had lost a lot of hair, it was falling out like crazy and was very annoying. Ben had hair in his sandwich today. Gross. I have enough to clean up after, I don't need to be cleaning up my hair all over the house. Besides, I couldn't do anything with it but wear it in a thinning pony tail.

So, for FHE (Family Home Evening) we gathered all the kids around and let them watch, comment, and make funny faces at me while Ben and Micah first cut my hair short, then buzzed the sides leaving a Mohawk, then buzzed it shorter and finally shaved it. Ben actually had a harder time with it than I did. While he was near tears at some points, I was usually laughing, until I saw him so sad. Then I wanted to cry, too. This is one of those times when it hits us how real this is. But I put on my high fashion model face and acted like this was a great adventure. The kids were fascinated. Chance loved the Mohawk and said, "Mom, you look like a dinosaur!" Benjamin said, "Your head is as smooth as a baby's bottom." At one point, I caught Morgen's eye. She looked terrified. She said, "Mom, you're still a girl like me, right?"

Today, I went on a walk with Naomi and Chance in the forest. Joseph was riding the dirt bike with Benjamin in the track. He saw us and stood up on a hill and yelled across the field, "Mom, Mom, Mom!"

"What?" I asked, thinking something was wrong.

"Are you still bald?" he shouted.

"Yup, yup, I'm still bald."

"Then show me your head!"

I took off my head scarf, letting my shiny scalp beam in the sunlight.

Joseph got a good look. "Okay!" Then he turned around and got back on his bike.

Well, either way, it's done now. My head feels light, and I can feel the air from the fan blowing around my ears and at the top of my head in a way I've never felt before. I still feel beautiful. It makes my ears stick out funny, but it makes my eyes look bigger and brings more attention to my facial features. Ben says I'm beautiful and told me how he loves how pretty my eyes look now. But it's still pretty crazy. He never thought he'd be shaving his wife's head, and I never thought it would be so funny to me. Just another example of the highs and lows of this. We cry. We laugh. We fear. We hope.

I feel beautiful. Yes, I'm bald. No, I never thought I'd say that.

Tonight, as I tucked Chance into bed, he said, "Mom, I'm going to say a prayer for you that you will feel better and not be sick anymore."

"Thank you, Chance. That's very sweet."

"I'll also pray that you don't die from the cancer. Even the baby, too."

I gave him a kiss and went to the other children. Then I heard him tell Ben, "Dad, I did an extra thing to help Mom."

Tuesday, July 29, 2014

Morgen came up to me this morning as I was putting my makeup on. She reached up and rubbed the top of my scalp. "All my hair is going to fall out too now," she said matter-of-factly.

I told her, "No, sweetie, you're not sick like me. Your hair isn't going to fall out."

She rubbed the crown of my head. "But I want to be beautiful like you."

Friday, August 1, 2014

We got home from our second round of chemotherapy last night. Ben's parents are here watching the kids so I can rest. I felt more sure that things would be okay during this next treatment, but I was also dreading dealing with it all again, now that I know what to expect. The hardest part is that the entire three weeks after the first round, I never felt 100% well. I always had to deal with some side effect or another. I realize that's just how it's going to be these next twelve weeks and in the time after the baby is born. I won't be 100% me. That's hard to face, because there are so many things I want to do and be, but it is what it is. It won't last forever, but twelve weeks sure feels like it sometimes.

I'm sore now from the port placement surgery we did yesterday. The port is a small, round device that sits under the skin just beneath my collar bone. It has a small catheter line that runs into the main vein coming down from my neck and sits just above my heart. The port allows the chemotherapy to be administered more easily than with an IV or PICC line IV. It should make it more convenient for the future, but boy, does it hurt now! I can't turn my head to the left or pick up anything more than five pounds, and lying down on my pillow makes me want to scream. I feel like such a baby sometimes. At least that part will pass in a week or so.

We met with the high-risk oncologist at the University of Colorado Medical Center. She was awesome and so supportive of focusing on both my health and the baby's health. She said, "I want this to be a beautiful pregnancy and birth experience for you. The cancer we can kick right out of the picture." She explained she will be monitoring the baby every three weeks when we come up for treatment and will be monitoring the baby during the surgery herself with her nursing staff and the surgeon's staff both on hand in case anything goes wrong. She told me how important it is for me to take in lots of calories and drink plenty of water. If everything goes well, I should still be able to deliver with the midwives in Durango and even have a water birth. That makes me so happy, as if I still have an element of control over this situation.

Wednesday, August 6, 2014

I've decided I need to keep a list of all the awesome things people have done for me and add to it so I don't forget or leave anyone out. Because seriously, it's been amazing.

1. Ben, Micah, Dillon, Kelland, and my sister-in-law, Laura, with several of her girls and boys, shaved their heads to support me shaving mine.

2. Katy made me a breast cancer hope necklace and earrings.

3. People have given me books and resources.

4. Tons of cards, letters, emails, texts from hundreds of people.

5. Friends and family dropped everything to help with the kids.

6. Lydia set up crowdfunding, and dozens of people donated to help us with travel costs.

7. Ward made me freezer meals.

8. Friends dropped off flowers.

9. Old friends from high school are throwing a huge benefit concert for me to raise money.

Tuesday, August 5, 2014

My awesome extended family sent me packages and packages this week full of handcrafted origami cranes! 1000 in all! The cranes symbolize health and long life! The origami is beautiful, and I'm going to make a mobile for the baby with it to remember their love and kindness!

Saturday, August 9, 2014

What we learned today at the county fair: Morgen and cotton candy make a great combination, Joseph is stronger than wind, and bald heads burn fast.

Tuesday, August 12, 2014

Isolated.

That's how I've felt most of my adult life. Yes, I've had amazing people in my life, lots of support and great relationships, but I've always felt that my burdens were mine to bear alone. I've had a lot of loneliness even while surrounded by loving, good people, because I felt like no one really understood my internal struggles. I've always been one who felt I had to do it on my own.

This experience has shown me the true goodness of humanity. People are awesome. They've blown me away with their kindness, their selflessness, and their genuine love. I have felt an amazing amount of support that was always there, but I never really felt until now. I've learned to let go, to allow people to help me. My heart has opened up to trust others.

Friday, August 22, 2014

We returned last night from the third treatment. I slept for over fourteen hours and just now got up at noon. I think the children are tired of me being sick, especially the younger ones. They don't understand why I can't play with them, or read a book, or go on a walk. I will try to do those things later, but I just can't right now, and I hate that. They get upset that mom isn't around, so they act out more against Grandma and Grandpa and with each other, which is frustrating. I am grateful Tom and Ginger are patient with them, and I'm grateful for the sacrifices they made to come help us.

We saw baby Kiery yesterday. Kiery is what we're going to name her. Yes, it looks like a girl, which was a bit shocking at first because I was so sure it was a boy. But she is growing well and already at the 68% percentile at 20 weeks. Her heart is strong, and she looks to be developing healthfully. I love seeing her. It's the best present in the world.

Only one more treatment and then surgery. We met with the high-risk OBGYN at the University of Colorado Medical Center again yesterday. She's monitoring the baby's growth and development. She will be present with a full OBGYN staff during the surgery to monitor the baby. They said during the last mastectomy they did on a pregnant mom, they had to do two blood transfusions. It was because the surgery can cause a lot of bleeding, especially during pregnancy, which causes elevated blood levels. So I may need to be prepared for that. If I go into pre-term labor, they will give me medications to try and counteract that. If my blood pressure drops too low or the baby shows signs of stress, they may need to do an emergency C-section. We'll be at 26 weeks. That seems so early, and it is, but we should be far enough along to save her if that happens. I pray it doesn't. Most likely, everything will be fine. But it's crazy to have to consider these possibilities. I could wake up from the surgery and the baby will have been born, and neither Ben nor I will have been present for it. Then we'd have a tiny baby in the NICU for weeks. That would be hard, but I just have to have faith that the Lord will make it all work out in the end. He has guided and sustained us so far, so I need to remember to turn to him and trust his will.

That sounds so easy. It's not. Sometimes the enormity of it all, the incredible danger we both face just crashes down around me.

Other times, I'm just in go mode. I think, "I've got this covered. We've got our plan. We just have to get through it."

In both instances, I can often forget to turn to the Lord. Why do I do that? I know I'm not strong enough to do this on my own. Why do I think I can run my life and handle this without Him?

This experience has been incredibly humbling. It's one of those times when there is no other choice but to turn to Him, to realize I'm not fully in control of my life and never really have been. Learning to put myself completely into His hands will be one of the greatest blessings of my life.

Monday, August 25, 2014

It's one o'clock in the morning, and I'm bawling in the bathroom instead of sleeping. I don't want to do this anymore. I don't. I'm so tired of it. I just want it all to go away.

Everywhere I turn right now, I feel guilty. Guilty for burdening Ben and his parents and my friends. Guilty for making this hard on the kids. Guilty for my lack of self-control with my temper. I'm trying to be a good wife and mom, but I'm frustrated with the ineffectiveness of my efforts and how I let my anxiety control me.

I feel guilty about being so negative right now instead of grateful.

Saturday, August 30, 2014

Healing shouldn't come in the face of death,
But better for it to come then,
Then not at all.
I've been so alone, so afraid,
Consumed by own insecurities for so long,
A short, yet eternally long life time,
A gray cloud feeding from the streams of fear
That rise from my mind.
Why does facing the grave change anything?
Shouldn't I have set these things aside long ago?
Wasted time,
At times, lightning energy blinding,
At others, walls of clouding nothingness
Keeping me stuck,
Keeping me small,
Afraid to move,

Afraid to fall.
Someone once said we all have a journey to take.
Some face the battle's front, smoke and bombs and guns.
Some watch as their bodies betray them and decay.
Some live in the shadow of another's dysfunction,
At the end of an angry hand, or the tip of a violent tongue.
But I think the hardest journey any of us ever have to take
Is the one held deep within.
The one no one else ever sees
Or can ever know,
The silent struggling of the soul,
The choice to become more than what we are,
To rise above our thoughts, our perceptions,
The way we treat ourselves and the world.
Sickness has set a certain spotlight upon me.
Others want to see how I will rise above the challenge,
Or succumb to it all and fall,
But what they don't realize is that the greatest journey I ever have to take
Is the one within my own mind.
Overcome the shadow cast long by my negativity,
The sharp, critical knife I wield in front of me,
A vain effort to keep myself safe.
All the while, cutting down, hurting others,
And myself most of all.
Trapped by walls of guilt,
Barely able to see above it,
But knowing there has to be a better way
To be at peace with the world
And myself.
Trying now to break through it all
Because, as every heart deep-down knows,
There is only life to live.
Love is the light that can pierce through,
Release the pain,

Forgive the anger, the guilt, the hurt,
Let it disintegrate,
Like fog in the rising sun.
Why have I fought against love?
Sounds like such a hippie phrase,
But it is the balm
Every soul is craving.
Healing shouldn't come in the face of death,
But better for it to come then,
Then not at all.

Saturday, August 30, 2014, later the same day.

Can I just say I'm so done with having cancer? I don't want to do any more treatments. I don't want to do surgery. I don't want to feel sick anymore. I don't want people constantly asking me about it. I want it to go away. I want it to be something of the past already. Ah! I just want my life to be normal.

I think the middle of any trial is the hardest. In the beginning, there's the initial shock but also an overwhelming amount of support and a "roll up your sleeves and get it done" attitude. The end is relief and celebration that it's over. The middle is when you actually have to go through the actions to "get it done." It's the longest, and to me, the hardest part. I heard someone once say, "It's easy to be a starter. It's hard to be a finisher." That's because of all the work and discomfort that has to happen between the beginning and the end.

I don't want to be a whiner. I know I have to do this. I'm just really, really tired of doing it. I wouldn't be honest if I didn't say that. At least once. Okay, maybe more than once. No one wants to hear me complain, including myself. But I have to acknowledge it. This is really hard.

Several people have told me I'm their "hero" or their "inspiration." I want to tell them, "Thanks, but you have no idea what you're really saying." I'm not a hero, and if wanting to lie in bed all day and hide from the world is your kind of inspiration, then I guess I've got that covered.

It's funny how when something bad or difficult happens to you, you're suddenly interesting. People listen to what you have to say. They follow your Facebook posts. They read your blog or your book. I'm still the same person even though I have cancer. I know I've grown because of it. In some ways, I'm better, and in some other ways, probably not so much. But now there's a news anchor from CBS4 Denver who wants to do an interview with Ben and me. Because I got cancer while pregnant, I'm now somebody special. No one would have wanted me on the news before. I just hope I use these opportunities to do good the way the Lord wants me to. I recognize that this is a unique opportunity, and so I'm willing to take it and speak out and hopefully bless someone else's life.

Some cute things the kids have said:

Morgen said, "Mom, why don't you have pretty hair like me?"

Chance has prayed for me to get better and the baby to be healthy every day for the past three weeks.

Morgen and I were playing fairies in the forest. She said, "Pretend that you're the fairy princess. You have a long, sparkly blue dress and…" she turned, looked at me, and said, "Pretend you have hair, okay?"

Monday, September 1, 2014

There is a mom whose daughter died of breast cancer at 28 years old who wants to meet me. One of my friends on Facebook read my blog and shared my story with this mother, who is a family friend of theirs. The mother then read my blog and asked if she could meet me.

From what I know, her daughter's story is similar to mine. She was young and already pregnant when she was diagnosed with breast cancer. It was the same kind as mine. Unfortunately, hers had either progressed further than mine, or the timing wasn't in her favor. (The timing of my diagnosis and where I was in the gestation period was ideal for surviving breast cancer when pregnant.) You can't start chemo until the second trimester, so maybe she found out early in her first trimester and then had to wait 12 weeks or so before starting chemo, allowing the cancer to progress and spread to the liver. I'm not sure yet what her exact circumstances were, but I've heard stories of other women who had such experiences. Her baby survived, but she passed away shortly after delivery. The mother is holding an annual recognition for her.

I guess hearing about this mother has reawakened me to the truly life-threatening condition I face. I no longer feel that this cancer will claim my life. I'm pretty confident that I will beat it and go on to live a long cancer-free life. But if things had been just a little different for me, then my story could have been like her daughter's. I still wouldn't have changed a thing. It was never a question for me to keep this baby. I have never doubted my resolve to be willing to die if it meant the baby could live. But that doesn't mean I want to die, or that I want to leave my husband and children. I am so grateful for every moment that I have, and I want to carry that appreciation with me every minute of my life, no matter how long or short it is. I am grateful my prognosis looks so good right now. I am grateful my body is strong and healthy and has been able to recover so well from the chemo treatments, even though it hasn't been easy. I am grateful the baby is healthy and growing well. I cannot wait to hold her. My heart is full of humility. I don't feel that I am any better or different than anyone else. We don't understand why the Lord allows what he does to happen. Why was that mother taken while I get to stay? I will never know and can't even pretend to understand it. But I am grateful. And that gratitude is something I want to keep within me forever.

Monday, September 8, 2014

We are waiting for Ben's parents to arrive so we can make the trek back up to Denver. It's going to be a big week with appointments on Tuesday and Wednesday and treatment on Thursday. I'm not happy about leaving the kids so long. We thought about bringing them with us, but that is always so stressful. The kids don't sleep well, so we don't sleep well, and the car rides are, well, what you would expect with five young children in the car: "I need to go potty." "He's looking at me." "When are we going to be there?" "I need to go potty again!"

So, it is what it is.

Tomorrow, we're doing an interview with CBS News 4. That evening will be the benefit concert. I will see people I haven't seen in ten plus years. When I was younger, I would have these reoccurring dreams where people from all stages of my life came together in one place. Old friends from school would be there as well as distant family members. I always wondered why everyone had gathered together like that. I can't help but feel that this event is like the fulfillment of that dream. I never thought I would be pregnant, bald, and battling cancer at that reunion, though.

I am so grateful to all the people who have served and worked so hard to make this event happen. It will be wonderful, nerve-wracking, and beautiful all at the same time.

I also get to meet Katy, Kelland's fiancée, for the first time this week. We may be able to go to the temple and do baptisms, which will be wonderful. I've been wanting to go to the temple for months now. I just want that connection again with the things that are eternally important. I want to feel the Spirit and know that my life is in the Lord's hands. I want the peace that comes only in His house.

Jasmine is planning to come from L.A. to spend the week with us. It will be great to see her, but she just came down with mono, so she may not be able to come.

Ben and I are both anxious to get answers about surgery this week. We want to know why it's so urgent that we have the mastectomy now instead of waiting four months until after the baby is born. I need to know what to expect with the recovery and what kind of help I'm going to need.

The best part of these trips is the time I have with Ben. It is so nice to have the long drives together and uninterrupted conversations. We've grown so much closer through this experience, and I treasure the time we have together.

Thursday, September 11, 2014

Last chemo treatment while I'm pregnant today! I'm looking forward to a break from it for a while!

Baby girl is doing well. One pound, four ounces today!

Saturday, September 13, 2014

I'm feeling scared about our future and our finances with Ben wanting to be home. It makes me anxious and insecure and overwhelmed. I also feel helpless to fix the situation.

I'm worried about Ben's emotional health right now. We are both dealing with so much. I hope I can talk to him and ease his burdens as best I can.

Sunday, September 14, 2014

Ben took all the kids to church by himself so I can recover from this last chemo treatment. I should be sleeping, but I can't seem to. Too many thoughts in my head. And I want to catch up on what an amazing week it was.

Before I get to that, though, I've been thinking a lot about forgiveness. What is it? Just a decision? How do you forgive those who continue to hurt you and never ask for forgiveness? I've been making an effort to feel love and gratitude in my heart for those people. I am confident that love is the answer. I hope to fill my heart and mind with so much love that it crowds out everything else. No room for hate. No room for pain.

It won't change what others do. It will only change the way I react and the way I let it affect me. I don't want to live with a heart full of pain and fear. I don't want to worry anymore. There is only one person I can change: me.

So (deep breath) I will love people anyway. I will remember and recognize the good in others. I will fill my heart with love and gratitude for all the good in them, and there is much good. There is good in all of us. I will shift my perspective until genuine kindness and charity come naturally to me. This is probably the hardest thing I've ever had to do, way harder than fighting cancer even. It's looking my greatest weakness in the eye, my natural desire to hold a grudge, and changing it to something stronger, something humbler, something purer. I know the Lord knows all of our weaknesses. He sees our sins and the hurts we cause others, but He loves us anyway. He never retracts His love from us, regardless of what we do. I don't know how He does that. That is what I'm trying to learn, trying to emulate. It has to be possible. It *is* possible. I will work at it until I get there.

Now, I am praying desperately to be filled with God's love. If I can't feel love myself, then I pray that I will feel His love and that it will sustain me until I have the love myself. I want to understand Him. I want to be as He is.

This isn't some small thing to me. It isn't some nice wish. It is the greatest undertaking of my life. I stand at the bottom of the mountain, looking up at my Mt. Everest. Along its jagged paths and cliffs, I see the pain that wants to drag me back down.

All of these thoughts and fears and pains batter against me and whirl inside me. I want to curl up and hide in the snow, in my own white cave of hurt. Would it be justified?

My counselor said it is impossible to forgive while under attack. She gave an example of someone hitting you. You want to forgive them, but they're still hitting you. She says it's impossible to forgive when you're still being hit. That's the natural response. The person has to stop hitting you before you can forgive them. But what if they never stop hitting you?

The Savior forgave even while he was on the cross. He forgave those who ridiculed Him, those who tortured Him, and those who killed Him. He did it even during the act of His torture. Did He possess some power we don't? There are many examples in the Bible and the Book of Mormon of men and women who forgave in the same manner. Moroni had a deep love for the

Lamanites even as they killed his people, which enabled him to quickly forgive them and allow them to go. The natural man would want to seek revenge upon them for all the wrongs they had done against them. Joseph forgave his brothers who sold him into slavery. Nephi "frankly forgave" his brothers who had tried multiple times to kill him. Joseph Smith did the same to the men who tarred and feathered him, ridiculed him, and tried to kill him. How did they do this?

The natural man justifies holding a grudge. But we are to put off the natural man. We are to become something more. I could go about my life, nursing wounds and never healing. Or I can choose to love.

Despite the winds and the cliffs and the pains that shake me, I see light at the top of the mount. It is the promise of peace. It is the promise of a life of love. It is freedom.

So, I will climb.

Part Three
Scars and Kindness

FRIENDS ARE FAMILY YOU CHOOSE

Monday, September 15, 2014

Ben and I went up on Monday. We got a call from Kathy Walsh of CBS4 News and met with her and her camera man on Tuesday morning. Ben and I were so nervous. That kind of thing is way out of our comfort zone. I strongly felt we could use this opportunity to do good. I really wanted to share the message that termination isn't the only solution for pregnant moms with cancer. Termination is the prevalent procedure in the Durango and Denver medical communities. I was told by multiple oncologists across the state that I was greatly risking my life by choosing not to abort. I wanted to challenge that message by showing it can be done. And as Dr. Borges says, "Choosing to terminate doesn't increase the survival rate at all."

With that message in mind, we did a thirty minute interview with Kathy Walsh. She asked a lot of hard questions about our faith: Why had we made the decision we did? How is it affecting the kids? How do we get through it? It turned out to be a really positive experience for both Ben and me. Ben was embarrassed a bit because the process caused him to cry, but I loved his raw emotion. He's been just as much a part of this as I have.

I was concerned people might see us as attention seekers, but I realized people are going to think what they're going to think. I know why I'm doing this, and it's for a good reason. I've always been a bold person. That's why I gravitated to the stage and performing arts. I've never been ashamed to stand up and bear my testimony and say what I think is right. I think if I didn't use this opportunity to do good, I would be missing some of the purpose of it.

The interview aired that evening on the five o'clock news. Of course, it was only a fraction of the full interview, but I hope it will help someone who may face a similar decision or at least help educate the medical community about other options.

We met with the plastic surgeon that afternoon and were not thrilled about the choices. That's putting it lightly. We were shell-shocked. Neither of us has been looking forward to surgery. It weighs on us for so many different reasons. First, it's my body, and it will never be the same afterward, which affects my self-confidence and has implications as far as intimacy. But even more than that, my breasts aren't just a cosmetic appendage. They're how I have nursed and nurtured my children and how I would like to in the future. I am grateful I don't have to have a double mastectomy, so I can still nurse with the one side, but it won't be the same. It may not seem like a big deal to someone else, but it is a big deal to me.

Then, there's the risk to the baby during surgery, and the possibility of an emergency C-section and waking up with a 27-week-old baby in the NICU. Not fun stuff to consider. Okay, terrifying actually. It's pretty rare for that to happen, and I don't feel that it will, but it's crazy that it's even a possibility.

And there's the recovery from the surgery. Two to three weeks of not being able to lift more than 10 pounds. Therefore, needing more help, and still being a burden. The stress it puts on the kids and the family. The effects of narcotics upon the baby.

So, with all these things already pressing on us, we met with the plastic surgeon. She showed us pictures of women who have had a mastectomy to prepare us. We were not prepared. They will remove all the tissue, including the areola, the nipple, and the lymph nodes. What is left doesn't look human. Even men have nipples. All that's left is a flat chest with red incision lines running along the bottom of what used to be the breast.

She explained that she will be unable to put the tissue expander in while I am pregnant, because it adds an additional hour to the surgery time, which puts the baby at greater risk. So, in order to have the tissue expander in place for a future implant, I will have to get it in the week the baby is born. It has to be that soon to allow the expander to slowly fill and stretch out my skin during the 12 weeks of chemo, and it has to be done before radiation. After radiation, I will have another surgery when they will put the real implant in place. Later, they will put on a nipple tattoo. Yeah. Really. That's going to be me.

So, I will be completely flat-chested for about five months; then 12 weeks of a slowly expanding tissue expander. Next, a fake boob that will have little physical sensation, will feel cold and hard, and will have to be replaced every 10-15 years. With a fake nipple.

Okay, so that might not all be so bad if the implant looks amazing, right? Ben and I were disgusted by the final results. You'd think plastic surgery would make it look pretty good, right? Not so from the pictures she showed us. They looked *awful!* Pink incision lines that never faded enough, no nipple, and then a fake one. It was shocking. So, right now, we are looking around for another plastic surgeon who may offer better results. It's funny to go boob shopping, but hey, I got to have something!

Enough about that. After our discouraging and somewhat shocking appointment with the plastic surgeon, we headed back to Littleton for the benefit concert. As I said earlier, I was nervous and excited to see people I haven't seen in 10-13 years. We walked into the high school's main hall, and tears immediately filled my eyes. Beautiful tables full of donated items for the silent auction filled the hall. Pink balloons rose into the air, and dozens of people were already lined up to buy tickets and bid on the items. We met Roland, my brother, for a few minutes before he had to go backstage and get ready to play his solo piano piece. I gave big hugs to people in line and to the three amazing friends who helped put the event together. It was incredible to see everyone again, even old boyfriends and people I hardly recognized anymore. I was so touched that so many people had come to support me.

We settled into our seats in the front row and were met with the most beautiful music. The Colorado Mormon Chorale opened with "The Sound of Music" led by my friend Joel Hillan. They were joined by Amy Stewart, one of my best friends from high school, who had gone on to pursue opera and music professionally. The choir was superb, and Amy's voice was absolutely incredible. I was in awe. Tears flowed freely. It was their love. It was the memories of standing on that stage myself singing those same lyrics. It was how I found myself in that place as a young girl, how I struggled then but how much joy there was too. It was life and how much it had changed since then, but also, how some things have stayed the same, like the people who matter most.

Amy shared her memory of the first day she met me. I stood on that stage that day and sang "Think of Me" while my father accompanied me on the piano. She said I was one of the kindest people she knew and that I never said a disparaging word about anyone. I didn't know she thought that of me. Jake Williamson, another great performer and friend, mentioned the singing master class I taught that led him to better his voice and pursue a career as a performer. Another dear friend told me privately how my friendship and genuine care for her had prevented her from taking her life when she was sixteen years old. Another told me how my good, quiet example led her to accept the gospel and be baptized into the church after high school. I was floored. I still am. I had never known the effect I had on others. As a teenage girl, I was often insecure and thinking mostly of myself. I tried to do my best to be a good person and love others, but I truly had no idea of the influence I had. I am grateful and humbled to learn of it now. And I'm not saying that to put myself up now, but to share that we never really know how much of what we do and say will affect others. We all have a great opportunity to do good or not. I hope to do good all my life. I want to be someone who builds others up.

Every person there that night was someone who sacrificed their time and energy to express love and support for me. That is what life is about. It's about loving and giving to others. Like the line from "Sixteen going on Seventeen," when Jen Over and Amy Stewart sang, "Love isn't love until you give it away."

The music was incredible and the images projected were beautiful, but it was the love shared that triumphed that night. It will echo in my heart for the rest of my life.

Words were inadequate to express my gratitude, my deep humility, and my love for those people that night, and they still are. It's one of those things that transcends speech but is something the soul understands.

Wednesday, September 17, 2014

"If you don't do surgery, you increase your chances of dying from this cancer threefold," Dr. Borges told us last week as we sat in the exam room. We wanted to know why it was so important to do the surgery now rather than wait until after the baby was born. We also wanted to know why doing further chemo and radiation after the baby is born was so important. The tumor has shrunk to the point where I can no longer see or feel it. It seems as though the chemo we've done has been enough to eradicate it. Of course, we couldn't tell on a microscopic level, but we were both feeling like maybe what we'd done was enough.

I wrote on August 22, 2014, "What if I can cure my cancer by the time this baby is born? What if, through exceptional nutrition, love and self-care, I can beat this? What if I don't have to go back for further treatment and radiation?"

That was my deep hope. But I knew I needed better understanding and to listen to Spirit. I was willing to accept whatever He prompted me to do, regardless of my personal desires.

Dr. Borges explained that at the beginning of her career, they only had Adriamycin and Cytoxan (the two types of chemo that I have had so far) to treat this type of breast cancer. Adriamycin and Cytoxan show great results initially, greatly reducing tumor size and spread. But within six months after such treatment, the cancer would return to a large number of patients more aggressively and would spread rapidly. Dr. Borges said that unfortunately, she had lost a number of young women to it. But things have developed greatly in its treatment in the past ten years. By combining Adriamycin and Cytoxan with radiation, anti-hormone therapy, and the other biological types of chemo I will get later, there is a 90% cure rate for my type of cancer. But I have to do the full process.

That process includes doing the mastectomy now, while I'm pregnant. Though the Adriamycin and Cytoxan have reduced the tumor noticeably, there are most likely still microscopic cancer cells in the tissue. If we leave it, it will feed off the pregnancy hormones, spread, and very likely become lethal in the sixteen weeks left until delivery.

We needed the medical answers as to why it was so important to go through with surgery and further treatment. I have those answers now, and it all makes a lot of sense, but it is still difficult to accept emotionally. I think I had an easier time accepting chemotherapy, even with its risks and difficulties, because I could see the end in sight. Providing everything goes well, there is an end date to treatment. But doing the mastectomy will change me forever. Even when the cancer is gone, my body will never be the same. Part of me will always be fake. Part of me will always be scarred.

Monday, September 22, 2014

Yesterday we had a BBQ with some friends. One friend told me, "Sorry if I seem awkward around you. I just don't know what to say… but know that I'm thinking about you and feel for you right here." She touched her heart. I told her, "Don't worry. Mostly, everything feels the same. Life is still life. We just have a few more things we have to do now." And for the most part, that is how I feel. Life is pretty normal. I wake up, get the kids' breakfast, exercise, do homeschooling, take a nap, write, play, clean the house, make dinner, put the kids to bed, and spend time with Ben. Yes, most of the things I do are the same. And yet, everything is different. Fears and worries frequently loom in the background for both Ben and me. Sometimes we address them head-on. Sometimes they linger like a shadow in the corners of our awareness. I catch simple moments in my consciousness and marvel at the beauty of life more often now. It's in Naomi's giggle at the dinner table as she throws a bit of food and looks to see our reaction. It's in Morgen's hugs at the end of the day. It's in Joseph asking me if I want to go play Ninjas with him. It's in Chance's beam of accomplishment as he falls off his dirt bike and stands it back up. It's in Benjamin's prayers that our home will be filled with the Spirit. These normal, everyday moments pierce me deeper now.

I was struggling with depression and anxiety pretty badly last week. I would feel dishonest if I didn't say that. I put on a smiling face and shield myself with bravery. But sometimes, our inner self knows our true emotions better than we do.

I found myself awake at six in the morning with tears streaming down my face because I had a nightmare that Ben had an affair with a beautiful woman with long hair and real breasts. I went for a walk as the sun rose over the mountains and treetops and couldn't stop the tears from falling. There are times when it seems this cancer has taken so much from me: time and energy, my health and my ability to be a mom all the time, my calling in the church that I loved so much, Ben's focus on work and career, and our time with our children, and now it's taking away part of my body too. I'm not worried about Ben's love or devotion to me. He has shown that his love transcends the physical and truly is eternal and enduring. Though my nightmares last week might seem to indicate it, I'm not worried about him having an affair. I think the dreams are showing me my fears about myself, my self-confidence, and my insecurities. I see what I once was and long for that. But it cannot be. I need to get to the point where my will to be here for my children and family and live a long and happy life is greater than my desire for a whole body. It's just something I'm going to have to do. But I want to turn it around into something that I choose to do. That perspective will make all the difference.

Wednesday, September 24, 2014

Ben and I went to a cosmetic surgeon here in Durango who was very highly recommended. We went to their office and looked at their breast reconstruction before and after pictures. The results were so much better than those we had seen from the cosmetic surgeon up in Denver. So, that was really encouraging. Seeing the mastectomy was still really hard, though. I actually started crying. I can't believe that's what I'm going to look like in just a few days. And I'll have to look like that for about 6 months. Am I superficial? Sometimes it feels that way. I don't know why the surgery is one of the hardest parts of this for me. I guess it's because it is permanent. I am confident that I will beat this cancer. I will look back and remember how hard it was to go through chemo, radiation, anti-hormone therapy, all the traveling, the stress, the worry, and the disruption to our lives, but I will remember it as something in the past. It won't stay with me. The loss of my breast will stay with me forever.

I will have to learn to love and accept my changed body. I will have to get to the point where I look in the mirror and don't cringe but see the beauty I possess.

I feel like I haven't been as connected to the baby as I would like. With my past pregnancies, everything was about the baby. This time, my mind has been consumed by so many things: cancer, treatment, the other five children, strained family relationships, surgery, and on and on. But this little person has been with me through it all.

I am going to make a conscious effort to give more thought and attention to her and to communicate my love and appreciation for her. She is incredible. What a strong little person to be willing to come to the earth under these circumstances! I want to be close to her. I want to enjoy this pregnancy and rejoice in this incredible gift I have been given.

I received another email from a friend on Facebook pushing me to try a natural cancer remedy. Every company and every professional thinks they have a cure for cancer. It makes them a pretty buck. Don't get me wrong, I fully believe in exceptional nutrition and using the plants and herbs Heavenly Father put on this earth for man's use. I am an avid exerciser and believe in the positive effects of exercise, healthy diet, and positive thinking on the body.

Many of the supposed "cures" are dietary lifestyles I was already living prior to my cancer diagnosis. And I still got cancer. I eat clean and consume very little processed food; I've nearly eliminated preservatives and additives from my diet. I aim to eat 70-80% raw or juiced fruits and vegetables. The rest is whole grains, lean protein, and the occasional treat. I love eating this way. My energy is awesome, and I have greater mental clarity. My moods are more stable, and I feel full of life. I know a diet high in nutrients supports the body and helps it heal itself. That is why I do it.

But I do not believe that diet alone is always enough. Half a dozen family members passed away from cancer because they chose to use "natural" cancer remedies vs. traditional western medicine. Several family members have cautioned me away from these methods. While they offer big promises, they often give little results. "You are gambling with your life," one husband told me. "I wish we had chosen differently."

People often become desperate when they hear the word "cancer." They grasp at anyone or anything that promises a cure. Navigating through the overwhelming number of methods and opinions was one of the most difficult things I had to do, especially since I tend to lean away from the standard American diet and medicine. The only way I could have confidence in the choices we made was with the Spirit. I know now that the Lord has guided our path and helped us navigate through it all safely. I do believe that he has inspired men and women to make the medical discoveries they have, and I've been surprised to learn that many of the medicines, even the chemotherapy drugs, are derived from plants and soils and other natural sources.

So, I fuel my body with exceptional nutrition to support my body and give my baby the best start possible. But I also use the best modern medicine available, because I don't want to be one of those people who died because they thought the natural cures would be enough. Maybe for some people they are, and that's fine. But I have never felt the Lord tell me that is the solution for me. The best solution for me is a combination of both.

Friday, September 25, 2014

At the benefit concert, I met the mother of a young woman who died from my type of cancer just after giving birth to her son. She was 28 years old and pregnant when she was diagnosed with cancer – so similar to me. But the timing of her cancer was different than mine. They found it at the beginning of the first trimester. They couldn't do chemo until she was twelve weeks along. In that time, the cancer spread to her liver. She was able to deliver her son, but she passed away shortly after that.

Just a few short weeks can make such a difference with this type of cancer during pregnancy. It makes me grateful for the timing of my diagnosis and treatment. If things had been just a little bit different, my story could have had an ending similar to hers. I am grateful to the Lord for prompting me and my caregivers to take quick action.

Dr. Borges said one of the dangers of breast cancer in young women is that the OBGYN or family doctors often dismiss the lumps or symptoms they find due to changes the breast tissue goes through during childbearing years, just as I had thought at first. I thought my lump was probably due to weaning from nursing and then becoming pregnant again. A lot of health professionals dismiss such a lump for the same reasons. Because it is so rare for young women to develop breast cancer, they don't encourage them to get further testing. Women don't get annual mammograms until 45. For all these reasons, breast cancer is often missed in its early and more treatable stages in young women.

According to the Center for Disease Control and Prevention:

Breast Cancer Statistics

Except for some kinds of skin cancer, breast cancer in the United States is:

- The most common cancer in women, no matter your race or ethnicity.

- The most common cause of death from cancer among Hispanic women.

- The second most common cause of death from cancer among white, black, Asian/Pacific Islander, and American Indian/Alaska Native women.

For more information, visit: https://www.cdc.gov/cancer/dcpc/data/women.htm – the Cancer Among Women page.

- In 2011 (the most recent year numbers are available)—

- 220,097 women and 2,078 men in the United States were diagnosed with breast cancer.*†

- 40,931 women and 443 men in the United States died from breast cancer.*†

I am so grateful my midwife didn't mess around with it but got me in quickly for an ultrasound. I remember the sonographer saying, "It's probably nothing to be concerned about, but I would like the breast specialist to take a look at it just to be sure." I'm grateful she didn't dismiss it either. The breast specialist looked at the ultrasound and decided right then to do a biopsy "just to be safe," even though he said that, "the probability of it being anything serious in a woman your age and in good health is so rare." Any one of these people could have dismissed it. I am so grateful that they did not. I hope a greater awareness develops and that preventive measures are taken by the medical community and young women themselves. It is rare. But it is deadly, especially for young women who are or can become pregnant while they also have hormone-positive breast cancer.

I am deeply grateful that my cancer was caught when it was and that everything has worked out as well as it has. My strength is returning after the last treatment, and the baby is growing and doing well. I love feeling her kicks and movements inside of me. My heart goes out to that mother who lost her daughter. I didn't have any words for her. It had to be painful to see me and relive memories of her daughter. Times like that make me realize again what a fine line we walk between life and death.

Sunday, September 28, 2014

Naomi and I have passed a lazy, rainy Sunday. Wish Ben had caught a video of me walking to the chicken coop as rain fell on my bald head!

Thank you to all the awesome people at Ignacio High School for making me this sweet poster!

Saturday, October 4, 2014

There is too much pent up within me. Too many fears. Too many realities I don't want to face. Surgery is in five days. We leave in four. This is the weakest I have felt so far. There was the initial shock, the scrambling for answers, the wading through decisions and consequences, starting and going through treatment, but I had a sense of inner calm and faith in what we were doing. Why has that left me now? Not that I've completely abandoned faith, it's just that I've let my fears overwhelm my thoughts and emotions. It consumes my energy. I feel weak and incapable of doing this.

I want to be strong. I want to have faith. I want to focus on the life this will give me rather than lamenting the things I'll lose. I just fear that I won't feel beautiful anymore. I'll look at myself and hate what I see. I haven't had a perfect body. It's gone through a lot of changes over the years with pregnancy and nursing. But even when I haven't liked the way I looked, I always felt that I had a beautiful chest and that made me desirable and encouraged me to work on the rest of me. Now, I won't have that anymore. It seems superficial and stupid. It makes me question myself. Where has my true value been all these years? In the superficial? In my own vanity? Who am I without my body? My beauty? What is my true worth?

I know logically I am more than my body, more than my breast. Of course. I know I mean more than those things to those who love me and to my Heavenly Father. I know that in the eternal perspective, this matters very little, but right now, it matters a lot to me.

I don't want to leave the children for five days. I don't want to be stuck drugged in the hospital for three days. I don't want to go through the pain and immobility for three weeks after, not able to lift my children or do all the tasks I am used to doing. I don't want to have to face the mirror, or try to put on clothes or feel ugly. Maybe it wouldn't be so bad if I could have reconstruction immediately after the mastectomy, even though that will never be as good as the real thing. The scarring and the fake nipple is just not something I'm looking forward to. I will be completely flat chested on one side for 18 weeks. I'm also big, pregnant, and bald. It's hard to feel pretty.

I'm venting. I'm lamenting, whining, despairing and giving voice to all the fears swirling inside me. It's not how I want to be, but it's how I am right now. I did a lot of work with Gina, my counselor, last week about drawing strength and healing from the positive memories of my past. I remembered the times when I felt completely capable, full of faith, full of love. She helped draw those feelings out of me until I felt their presence again in my awareness and my body.

They are tools I can use to help me in times of anxiety. I need to focus on the strength I have. I need to ramp up my faith!

Wednesday, October 8, 2014

I keep running this scripture through my mind, relying upon the Lord to get us through this.

Thursday, October 9, 2014

The day of surgery. It's 5:30 a.m. We need to leave in a few minutes to go to the hospital for surgery, but I just have to share the incredible amount of gratitude I feel in my heart this morning. I know the Lord is with me. I can feel His presence and His Spirit so strongly within me. I feel His angels close by. I looked in the mirror before I got in the shower, so grateful for the body I have been given. I am grateful for my life. I am grateful for this baby growing within me. I am grateful for Ben. He is and has ever been my rock. I am grateful for all those praying for us and loving us.

Surgery went well – no complications at all and baby is doing well. She's a little rock star! Thank you all for your faith, prayers, and love. I felt the Lord so close to us today, and I know He is watching over us. We're gratefully resting and recovering now.

Saturday, October 11, 2014

We're home now. We were discharged from the hospital mid-morning yesterday because everything went so well. When the surgeon came into the room after the surgery to check up on me, she said, "Wow, you look really good." I wondered, "Really? What should I look like?" She said that her last pregnant mother to undergo a mastectomy had to have two blood transfusions, was throwing up everything, and was in incredible pain despite the narcotics. Made me realize it could have been a lot worse and that the Lord had really sustained us through it. The baby did great during the surgery. I didn't have any major contractions. The blood loss was minimal, and they got it done in about two and a half hours.

They brought Ben in after I woke up in the recovery wing. I was pretty tired still, but it was so good to see him. He had waited over four hours! His brother Josh had come early that morning from the Springs and spent the entire morning with him. I was so grateful he had company during that time. Then they wheeled us up to the seventh floor to a private recovery room. We were originally going to recover on the labor and delivery floor, but it was full. It was fine, though, because I liked where we were. It was quiet. The nurses monitored my vitals, and the OBGYN staff came in that night and then again in the morning to monitor the baby. We both did great, so the OBGYN staff and surgeon gave us the all clear to go yesterday. We were so grateful to be able to get back home and get some real rest, because the night before, the nurses were in our room every hour all night long checking on us.

We brought a dump trailer full of wood out to Ben's parents and then headed home. I slept most of the way; Ben struggled to stay awake because he had slept so little, but he got us home safely around midnight.

Amy said all the kids did great. She was certain there were angels attending them, giving her strength and patience and helping the kids do so well at getting along and being obedient. I checked on each of them, tucked them in, and then happily went to sleep in the comfort of my own bed.

I slept in late this morning and then went out to say hi to the kids. They gave me gentle hugs and asked to see what the doctors had done. We brought them all into my room and explained it to them again. We told them what the drainage tube coming out of my skin and hanging out my shirt was for and that my body didn't look the same anymore. I told them it was a little gross looking and that they didn't have to see it, but they could if they wanted to. They all did, and I felt that it was better for them to see it than to imagine something worse. So I pulled back the bandages and showed them the incision. It's about 4 ½ inches long, and the skin around it is all loose and wrinkly so that there will eventually be room for the implant. Zarah, my niece, said "It looks like grandma skin."

Their little faces were full of concern and a little disgusted. But I let them take their time asking questions. Did it hurt when they did it? Did I see them take the breast out? Did it hurt the baby? Where is the breast now? Will I still be able to nurse with the other breast? After I had answered their questions, Benjamin said, "I'm sorry you have to have cancer, Mom." Morgen said again, "When I'm a Mom, I'll be bald." Joseph kept checking on the blood draining from the tube and the strap of the bag I use to hold it. He said, "When Morgen is an adult, she'll have a big chest, right?" I told him yes. "But I won't because I'm a boy, right?" I reassured him again. He seemed satisfied with that.

I can tell they are concerned and thinking about it, so I'm trying to be really open and answer their questions and assuage their concerns. Benjamin sang a little song that had the words "No more Denver, no more Denver" in it when he learned we wouldn't have to go up there again until after the baby was born.

I absolutely felt the Lord's presence with us this week. I felt His angels with us, especially when it was time to say goodbye to Ben and they wheeled me back to the OR. I knew there were some special spirits with me and all of us, giving us strength, comfort, and faith. I never felt alone. I know He helped everything go as well as it did.

I've been resting a lot today. I slept about five hours and have mostly been sitting around, talking with the kids and playing with Naomi some. I can't pick up anything more than 10 pounds for a while, so I can't even pick Naomi up, but Ben and Amy have been taking care of all that. I'm only taking one Percocet every six hours, when I could take two every four hours. I've been doing that since Thursday afternoon, the afternoon after my surgery, when I decided to stop taking the IV meds. My pain levels have been easily managed at that dose, and I feel better about its effects on the baby. I've noticed she has been less active than normal, and that's probably because the narcotics make her sleepy. I'm grateful Mark and Amy are here to help us out and for Ben's help too. I feel like this is the last really big hurdle, and we're getting through it well.

Sunday, October 12, 2014

I'm feeling pretty useless right now. There's not much I can do with the kids or around the house even though I want to. It's frustrating. I feel like I should be doing something.

Things aren't going so well at the shop right now, and that is worrisome to both Ben and me. The guys haven't supported Mark as manager, which is frustrating because he only came in to help Ben get us through this rough time. I think we are both feeling a bit overwhelmed and directionless. I need to turn the matter over to the Lord and let His Spirit guide both Ben and me. But I'm worried about Ben. There's so much on his plate right now, and these issues with the employees only add to that. The problem with Autocrafters is that it always sucks all his energy, and then we get into survival mode and don't work on our dream of being financially free and owning multiple businesses and rental properties. I feel like we have some serious thinking, praying, and pondering to do to get us refocused on what it is we really want. I know it will work out in the end, but right now, it's pretty stressful.

Today I'm seeing how I do on only Tylenol. Already, my mind feels clearer, but I'm not sure if that's really the best thing for me, because then I feel like I should be doing things, and it's hard to force myself to rest. I do feel better about it for the baby though.

Thursday, October 16, 2014

Today I realized how grateful I am I can shave my legs. I've never been particularly grateful for that, but after a week of not being able to even wash my own feet, it felt like such freedom! Life is so much sweeter when we appreciate the little things! Grateful to the sweet Relief Society sisters for the delicious thanksgiving dinner they provided us this week!

Saturday, October 18, 2014

A Real Love Story
"Good morning, Smoe."
Smoe short for Smorgeous.
Smorgeous because it rhymes with gorgeous.
Gorgeous.
He thinks I'm gorgeous.
But I look in the mirror and an alien looks back at me.
Pale skin, dark circles under eyes,
Stubby hair shorter than all my boys,
Swollen, pregnant belly.
Lift the bandages,
One breast,
One jagged red scar cutting through wrinkled skin across a flat chest.
Who is this person?
"You are beautiful."
He kisses the top of my fuzzy head.

Beautiful,
That word does not mean what it did a week ago,
Beautiful.
The curves have morphed, body deformed.
Once smooth skin, soft and pure,
Now running in jagged lines of red.
The curls of last year fallen to the floor and swept away.
Face ashen, lacking the summer sun's kiss.
No clothing fits.
All the hats itch my head.
I throw my Sunday dresses on the floor
Because they fit a person I'm not anymore.
Smiles and golden hair glare at me from the pictures on the walls of our home,
The fairytale princess, but the lilies of our wedding day have long since faded,
And they're thrown away.
And he tells me I'm beautiful.
Beautiful.
And it makes me think, through the tears that cloud my eyes,
That word means more now than ever before.
It's changed.
Just like me.

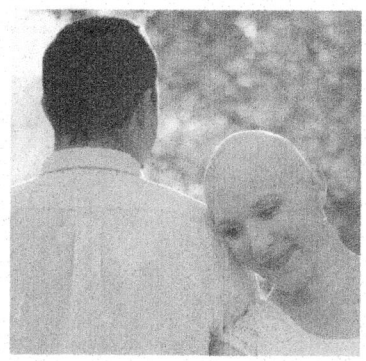

And now I know just what he meant every time he said it before,
So much more than lipstick and perfume,
So much more than youth and skin.
More than fleeting feelings,
Heightened, but temporary emotions
That are as fleeting as the summer sun.
So many base their love upon these,
But not him.
Even as mutilated as I am, he holds me,
He lets me cry,
He tells me I'm beautiful,
And I believe him
Because love and beauty are more than words or images.
Beauty is carved by years of dedication,
Of selfless, enduring devotion,
And no scalpel can take that away.
And love is more than butterflies and flying on cloud nine,
It's catching one another as the storms pound
And threaten to plunge us to the ground.

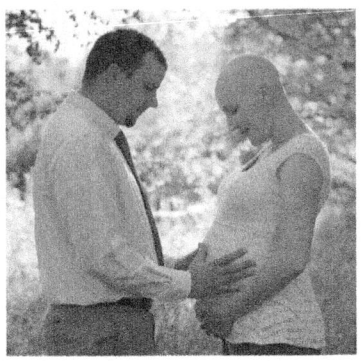

Love is more than emotion.
It's the steady hand that never lets go
Come rain, or scars, death or pain.
It's more than a knight in a fairytale.
It's waking up in a hospital bed, when everything feels like it's fallen apart,
Looking into his eyes and hearing these words,
"Good morning, Smoe."

Tuesday, October 21, 2014

Dr. Finlayson called us with the results of the mastectomy after the lab had had a chance to test and study all the tissues and lymph nodes. The great news was that all my lymph nodes were clear of cancer. There were no growing tumors or any presence of cancer cells in them. This is a relief to hear, because it means we don't have to go back in for immediate surgery to remove more lymph nodes. I've really had enough of surgery right now. The other good news was that there were no infiltrating cancer cells present. Those are the ones that spread beyond the breast tissue. All had been destroyed by the chemotherapy! They did, however, find ductal carcinoma tumors still present. Those are the cancer cells that form in the breast but stay within the milk ducts. But they had removed all the breast tissue, and therefore, all the ductal tumors.

I may be completely cancer free right now! Of course, that's my hope, not something they said. They won't know if there is cancer in my body until after the baby is born and we can do the scans. Even then, I guess I'll never hear them say the words, "You're cancer free." But I can hope.

And right now, I'm hoping I truly am cancer-free, so when we do the scans after the baby is born, we'll find no growing tumors. Then perhaps I won't have to do any more treatment. I'm sure that's not what Dr. Borges and the other oncologists will recommend, but it may be something I will choose to do. The breast is gone. The breast cancer tumors are gone from the left side.

I would be thrilled if I could put this in the past and move on with my life. Either way, I'm making sure to get optimal nutrition and take good care of myself for my health and the health of my baby. I'm going to give us my best shot.

Wednesday, October 22, 2014

I've decided to embrace my early morning wakefulness as a time to quietly meditate, ponder, and pray. It is a wonderful time to connect with the Spirit, analyze myself, and think about who I really want to be, who God wants me to be, and how I can rely more fully upon Him to change my thoughts and behaviors.

I am so grateful for this time of quiet reflection, which is so scarce during the day with the noise and needs of the children. I enjoy the peace and am grateful for the clarity I receive.

Here is what I received this morning:

- Pray aloud when disciplining the children, when my temper is up and frustrations come. I know this seems silly, but I'm going to give it a try. I need to stop, not act, and be like the Anti-Nephi-Lehies, pouring out my soul to God for strength, patience, and help and be grateful that my children will see me faithful, humble, and strong amidst the fiery darts of the adversary.

- Don't excuse my emotions or run with them. Emotions can be changed. Pray until my emotions change and my thoughts and behaviors are in line with who God wants me to be.

- Pour my whole soul into converting my children to the Gospel.

- Listen to the Spirit. Pray throughout the day.

- Replace fear, panic, and anxiety with FAITH by turning my will and my life to God.

- Show gratitude for others.

- Happiness comes through service and sacrifice.

Today was amazing. I did as prompted and said a prayer out loud before the children multiple times when there was contention and once when I felt frustration. I felt the Spirit so much more. I spoke and acted in a kinder and more nurturing way. And the children responded so well to it.

I prayed more in my heart throughout the day as well, and felt more peace, clarity, and direction than I have in a long time, if ever. This is key for me. I must remember to do this – to pray until I feel, think, and act like the person I want to be, like the Savior. I am very grateful for the direction I received and feel confident that I can repent, receive a remission of my sins, and become like Christ.

Thursday, October 23, 2014

I'm pretty well recovered from the surgery now. The incision line looks pretty good. It's just a thin, pink line. But my skin is all wrinkly and weird looking with nothing plumping it out. I've come to a measure of acceptance about it now. I can even laugh about it. I never thought I'd be stuffing my bra at 29. I look in the mirror, and I don't recognize the person looking back at me. My hair is about a quarter inch long and looks like a boy's buzz cut. It's all fuzzy and sticks out all over. My belly is swollen, and I have one breast. I never in my life thought I'd look like this.

Friday, October 24, 2014

I've really been working on improving my thoughts and behaviors. I truly believe we are the creators of our own lives and our own happiness. I love this quote from Will Smith, "Talent you have naturally. Skill is only developed by hours and hours and hours of beating on your craft…. Where I excel is ridiculous, sickening work ethic. While the other guy is sleeping, I'm working. While the other guy is eating, I'm working."

Time is short. We never know how long we have. Why should I put off being the person I want to be and living the life I want to live?

Here are the things I'm working on:

1. I am loving, patient, and soft-spoken.

2. I am a #1 New York Times Bestselling Author by May 1, 2016.

3. I earn Napoleon Hill passive income from my book sales by May 1, 2015.

4. I publish five Jonas Flash books by August 1, 2015

"I believe I can create whatever I want to create… The first step, before anyone else in the world believes it, is that you have to believe it. There's no reason to have a plan B, because it distracts from plan A."
—Will Smith

I've been doing incredible visualization exercises daily where I think of positive, happy experiences from my past and project those emotions toward the success I want to have. I feel as though I have already accomplished the thing that I desire. Then I accept it into my life and release it. It has already had a powerful effect upon me the past three or four days. I have felt more love, peace, faith, and happiness inside me, and it has permeated all I say and do. I truly have had more patience. I've been able to stop during times of anxiety or frustration and feel peace and speak softly. I feel like I've really found something that is going to change my life. I will be the person I want to be.

Saturday, November 1, 2014

12 Things I Wish I Knew Before I Got Breast Cancer

1. WHEN IN DOUBT, CHECK IT OUT.

For over three months, I had noticed a lump developing in my left breast before I saw my physician. If I'd known then what I know now, I wouldn't have waited to get it checked out – I would have gone at the first suspicion that something might be wrong with it. I thought it was part of the changes in my breast tissue happening as I was weaning my daughter. I dismissed it until it grew too large to ignore. I'm one of those people who doesn't want to make a big fuss over things. I don't want to go to my doctor for every little bump or bruise and waste their time or mine. I don't like looking like a paranoid idiot. Well, now I know it's better to look like a paranoid idiot than to allow a real life-threatening condition to progress unchecked. So now I know, when in doubt, check it out. It won't hurt you, really.

2. HEALTHY EATING IS IMPORTANT, BUT IT'S NOT A PANACEA.

I am such a firm believer in eating a diet rich in whole, unprocessed foods and consisting primarily of raw fruits, vegetables, and nuts. I have seen what a difference this way of eating has made in my life, my energy levels, my skin, and my weight, and I am so grateful for it. When I found out I had breast cancer, however, I was pretty angry. Wasn't I doing all the things that were supposed to prevent this sort of thing? Why hadn't it been enough? What had I done wrong? Weren't all of my sacrifices worth anything? I've since come to understand that healthy eating, although so important to our health and happiness, isn't a panacea. It cannot always prevent us from developing cancer or disease. Sometimes we have to use alternative measures to heal our bodies and save our lives. I'm more at peace with that now. But I will always use food as my first medicine.

3. ABOVE ALL, TRUST YOUR INSTINCTS.

This was one of the hardest things to do, but it gave me the most peace as we tried to navigate through the conflicting opinions, advice and options. It is difficult to listen to the well-educated, professional opinion of a doctor or medical professional and tell them no, you won't be doing what they recommend. But it is so crucial. Especially as a mother who has been given a divine right to receive revelation for the care and nurturing of her children. If I had not trusted my own heart, I would have followed the doctor's strong urging and aborted my baby. I wouldn't be 30 weeks pregnant now with a strong, healthy baby girl while still on my way to making a full recovery. That would have been a decision I would have regretted forever. Even members of my family were pushing me in that direction. I had to stand strong despite it all. We all have one life to live. What is it worth if we can't live with the person we've become?

That was the biggest decision. I had to follow my own heart. But the idea of trusting your instincts came up again and again throughout my treatment. It came up when deciding who I would allow to watch my children, choosing to homeschool or not, choosing to get a morphine shot before surgery in case the baby was taken early, and so many other things. Sometimes, it was simply following the instinct to gather more information before proceeding with a procedure or taking a medication.

My oncologist told me that the biggest reason breast cancer is so deadly in young women is because health professionals dismiss their concerns over finding a lump. The patients believe them, and they don't get it treated until it is too late. Seeking a second, third, and fourth opinion is crucial if your instincts are telling you something the doctors are not.

4. CANCER KILLS. DO EVERYTHING YOU CAN AND FEEL YOU SHOULD TO FIGHT IT.

I have been approached by more people who told me their loved ones passed away because they didn't utilize the resources and treatments available to them than by those whose loved ones survived using this mentality. Most of these deceased loved ones tried to go the purely natural route to cure their cancer. I've only met one woman who has been able to keep her cancer at bay using nutrition and homeopathic methods, but she didn't have breast cancer, and every type of cancer is different.

Previous to having cancer, I felt I would never do chemo or radiation if I ever got it. I was a firm believer that God provides us with the plants and herbs we need to cure disease. I now believe that no treatment method should be ruled out when your life is on the line. I know God also inspires men and women to make incredible advances in the science and medical fields, and we should not ignore these.

I've looked into the face of a mother who lost her daughter, a husband who lost his wife, and seven children who lost their mother, all because they refused to utilize the treatments and resources available to them. But ultimately, it goes back to trusting your instincts. Only you can know what you can and cannot live with. If you cannot live with the fact that you used chemo to cure your cancer, then don't. But don't be one of those women buried in an early grave if you don't have to.

5. HAIR IS JUST HAIR. DON'T STRESS TOO MUCH ABOUT IT.

I always felt this was one of the most superficial aspects of my journey, and I guess it was, but that doesn't mean it didn't have its place. For me, it's one of the things I would like to go back and tell my pre-cancer self: "Stop worrying about so much!" Before I got cancer, I put too much energy and thought into my hair. I've always wanted to look my best, but I think I had an unhealthy obsession with my hair. It was actually really freeing to shave it off. I learned I am still beautiful, even bald. I realized how much time I spent trying to get my hair to look perfect every day, and how trapped I was in thinking there was only one way I could look attractive.

I am going to be much more adventurous and care-free about my hair in the future. Right now, it's just fuzzy stubble on my head. It sticks out everywhere, and I can't do anything with it. I love it. It looks like a buzz cut I would give my boys, and for some reason that makes me smile every day.

6. EVERY DAY REALLY IS PRECIOUS.

We all know this. We've all heard this. I remember hearing a thousand times before how life was a gift and that we should appreciate each day. But going through this process impressed that reality into my heart. We truly don't know how much time we have. Cancer could take us in a year, or a car accident could take us tonight. We live with the illusion that we have lots of time still ahead of us. What person doesn't imagine themselves growing old and living a long, full life? But it doesn't always work out that way.

Before, I spent so much of my time thinking about the future or the past more than the present moment. I'm very goal-driven, and I think most of my focus was on what I wanted to achieve rather than on being grateful for and enjoying what I had in the present. I still believe in bettering ourselves and aiming to improve our lives and realize our talents, but I also appreciate the present moment more. When I heard the words, "You have breast cancer," the world suddenly became very small. I realized how unimportant so many of things I'd been working on were and what the most precious things to me are. Now, I make space in my awareness and day to enjoy the little awkward and often humorous moments of life. I appreciate my children more, my husband more, and all the incredible blessings the Lord has given me.

7. DON'T PUT OFF BEING THE PERSON YOU WANT TO BE.

We all have things we know we need to improve on, those flaws in our characters we know need to change. Why then do we seem to allow the mundane routines and busy-ness of life to prevent us from actually working on them? At least that's what I did for most of the past ten years. Some of the biggest things I knew I needed to work on were my temper, my impatience with the children, my pride, my criticism and judgment of others, and my unwillingness to forgive those who hurt me. After I found out I had cancer, the stabbing realization came to me that I might not have as much time as I thought to work on these things. What if I'd had a year or less before I was called home and had to stand before my maker and be accountable for the things I had done? I became desperate to overcome those weaknesses and finally be the person I really want to be and that the Lord expects me to be. Nothing else was more important. The progress I've made in these past months has been amazing, and all because I've really dedicated my effort to it. It truly is amazing what a person can do when they put their will to it.

I'm not willing to waste any more time in making changes within myself. I'm still not perfect, and I still struggle, but at least I won't allow procrastination to be added onto the pile. I am 100% dedicated to being the wife, mother, daughter, and person I want to be, and that is something I live with every day.

8.   FORGIVENESS SHOULD BE GIVEN, NOT EARNED.

I touched on this in the last section, but this is such a big thing to me that I
need to give it more attention. Like I mentioned, forgiving those who have
hurt me was something I knew I needed to do but hadn't been able to master.
Okay, I wasn't even close to mastering it. I still felt pain, hurt, justification for
distancing myself, and an edge of resentment. And the hardest part was they
continued to do and say the things that had caused me and my husband so
much pain to begin with! I struggled with knowing I needed to forgive them
without actually knowing how to do it! How do I forgive them when they
continue to hurt me? How do I forgive someone who doesn't say sorry, isn't
repentant, doesn't seem to be willing to acknowledge or admit their hurtful
behavior, and doesn't seem to have any desire to change?

I really wanted to forgive. I wanted to let go of the pain. I didn't want to
carry bitterness in my heart. I wanted to fill my heart with love, not anger
and resentment. Every time I felt I was getting close, they would do another
hurtful thing, and I'd be right back where I started. But I wanted to be free of
this. I knew how the Savior forgave those who tormented him, ridiculed him,
and hurt Him. I knew how Nephi "frankly forgave" his brothers for all the
injustices they did against them. I knew how Joseph Smith forgave those who
tarred and feathered him, sought to kill him, and mocked him. If these people
could extend forgiveness like that, then I knew I could too.

I turned to the scriptures and to the words of the modern prophets, watched
every "Mormon Message" video on forgiveness, and prayed. I prayed
desperately and earnestly. I prayed to have the love of the Savior in me so
that I could know how to forgive. I came to understand forgiveness is a choice.
It's as simple as that. And if it is a choice, then why should I waste any time
in making it? Why not free myself of the burden now instead of carrying it
with me for years? Years I may or may not have. I realized forgiveness wasn't
something that had to be earned. It was a gift. And I had the power to give it.

It didn't happen easily or quickly. It took time and a never-ceasing desire to obtain it. I prayed day after day for months. I prayed that love would fill my heart, and I would choose love over everything else. That wasn't to say what had been done was okay. It didn't mean I would roll over and allow the poor behavior to continue. On the contrary, I took stands and set boundaries to protect myself and my family. I realized I might never hear the apology I so desperately yearned for. I might never have the relationship I wanted and felt I deserved. But I could forgive. I could focus more on loving others than condemning them. I could love them *despite* the things they did to me. I can honestly say now I do have more love in my heart than resentment. I have more peace than pain.

Turning to the Savior and allowing His love and atonement to work in my life has given me the room within to love and forgive.

9. GET THE BEST MEDICAL CARE POSSIBLE. YOUR LIFE IS WORTH THE COST.

I am a scrimper at times. Maybe not when it comes to the pair of new boots I really want, but I am when it comes to some things, like medical costs. That just seems like an extra expense on top of everything else. I know, great priorities, right? I learned, however, that there are times when it is worth the extra cost and sacrifice to get the best care. I found the best care for me and my baby 300 miles away from our small town in Southern Colorado at the University of Colorado Medical Center, not at our local hospital, where they didn't have the expertise my case required. This decision cost us a great deal more time and money, but it was worth it.

10. BE WILLING TO ACCEPT OTHERS' HELP.

I am a do-it-yourselfer. I made the choice to have five children (soon to be six), and that's not something most people choose. I felt like I needed to take responsibility for that choice. I'd been resistant in the past to allowing others to help me watch the kids, bring me meals, clean, or anything else that I felt fell into "my territory." I was super uncomfortable accepting others' help, because it made me feel less adequate somehow.

I've learned just how false that is. Allowing someone to help me doesn't mean I'm not capable. It doesn't make me any less of a person or mother. If anything, it shows confidence in myself and openness to the kindness and generosity of others. It shows a soft and receptive heart. One of the most spoken words in the scriptures is "receive." The Savior asks us to "receive His spirit," "receive His atonement," "receive His gospel," and on and on. Being able to receive truly is a Christ-like virtue.

I could not have received the care I needed without the help and generosity of others. Family and friends came and helped watch the children. People made us meals and freezer meals so I wouldn't have to cook. Women from my ward came every Friday and cleaned my house. Hundreds of people donated money to help us with our travel and medical costs. My friends held a benefit concert for me. People shared my message and helped me find resources. They sent cards, emails, and texts with words of encouragement and support. And on and on.

This has taught me that we really need one another. Accepting others' help blesses their life as well as mine. And now, instead of feeling uncomfortable, I am so deeply grateful.

11. DON'T BE AFRAID TO SHARE YOUR STORY.

I believe one of the reasons why this happened to me is because I can use my experience to help others and share the messages of Christ's gospel. But that doesn't mean I have always wanted to or that it's been easy. One of the hardest things to do was to allow Ben and myself to be filmed for an interview with CBS4 News in Denver and share our story with them. I was worried people would see me as trying to get attention from it, or that we were using a tragedy to line our pocketbooks or something like that. Cancer is a very private thing. It was scary opening ourselves up and talking about it. But I set aside those things, because I felt there was an important message I needed to share. I wanted other mothers like me to know that it was possible to keep your baby while fighting breast cancer and that abortion wasn't the only option. Currently, much of the medical community in Denver recommends abortion as the best option for treating a pregnant woman with cancer. It is a great misunderstanding. I wanted to share the message that a woman can fight cancer while pregnant and that both she and the baby can get through it healthfully.

So we let the cameras roll and answered the news anchor's questions; we were as open, honest, and transparent as possible. I have also shared our story through my blog, on Facebook, and through the book that I am writing. I don't feel keeping this experience or the lessons I've learned a secret will do anyone any good, and that includes me. We all go through hard times. How much better off we'd be if we could learn from one another!

12. TRUE LOVE STICKS IT OUT IN THE GOOD TIMES AND THE BAD.

I used to believe that love was that happy, fluttery feeling you got in your stomach when you thought of or were around someone you loved. True, that is a part of love, but it is far from the depth of real love. I have learned that real love is more than any feeling or emotion, because those things change with time. If love is based on the way that we "feel" for someone else, then as soon as we feel differently, that relationship is over. No wonder so many people divorce and separate because they "fell out of love," or just "don't feel the same as they did when they first got together."

Real love is dedication. It is service and sacrifice. It is putting another's needs before your own. It is giving without any thought of receiving in return. It lasts through poverty and wealth, through sickness and health, in the good times and the hard times.

I have been blessed with a husband who has given me that kind of love. He has loved me when I was too tired and sick to get out of bed for days and days. He has loved me when my hair fell out and my breast was removed, leaving my body scarred and deformed. He has loved me when I broke down and cried and cried because I just couldn't take it anymore. It would have been easier for him to pull away, or to busy himself with work and other distractions to keep him from his fear and lessen the pain of potentially losing me, but he didn't. He stood by me. He sacrificed work and sleep, time and energy to serve me. He gave everything within him in prayer and fasting for me. He stood by me when it would have been easier to walk away. I have learned from him what love really is and how it is possible to have love for decades in this life and for all eternity.

Saturday, December 20, 2014

Just days away from delivery now. I feel huge, anxious, and excited all at once. I haven't written lately because it was so nice to set everything down for a while. I had several weeks where I could just focus on this pregnancy and not have to worry about traveling, treatment, and all that. We fell into our more normal routine, and it felt like it was pretty much back to the way it used to be. Ben went back to working full weeks. I homeschooled the children and worked on my books. The only time I needed to go to the doctor was for my prenatal check-ups.

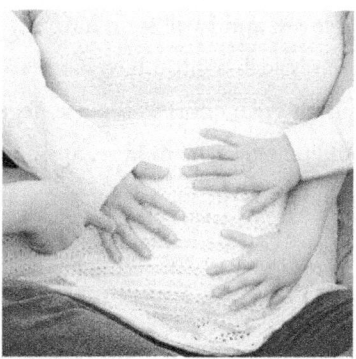

We have to pick it all up again now. It's caused me a lot of anxiety these past weeks, and I've worked really hard to ease that and return to faith and calm, but it's a struggle. The birth of this baby is an exciting, incredible blessing, but unfortunately, it also ushers us back into facing the cancer issues as well. It doesn't feel very fair to this baby, and I'm trying to separate the two in my mind. I feel like her birth is a point on a mountain. We find out the effects of all the treatment at the moment of her birth, and we start the second half as well.

It's easy to feel overwhelmed as I imagine trying to meet the demands of having five children along with a newborn baby and undergoing more chemo and radiation for the next year. Our newborns alone have been very demanding and have provided some of the most difficult experiences of my life. They have suffered from colic and have tended not to sleep well until about six months of age. That means long nights and tired days, and now I'm supposed to go in for chemo treatment every three weeks for the next year. I feel inadequate and worry that I might not be able to handle it all. Sometimes it's hard enough just to get through the day with the children as it is!

When I start feeling anxious about these things, the only thing I can do is pray to the Lord for strength and help. I recognize how much He has blessed and sustained us this far, and I have faith that He will continue to do so. It also helps me to focus on the tremendous blessings I have: I am still alive, the cancer seems to be going away, and I will soon have my beautiful, precious daughter in my arms. That is such a gift. I have no reason to worry or complain. So, I'm expending great effort to replace negativity with gratitude and fear with faith. I could play the victim here, and sometimes I do, but that won't serve me in the end. This is the lot I've been given. Now, it is my choice as to what I'm going to do with it.

I've been doing a lot of relaxation, meditation, and visualization these past few weeks to prepare myself for labor and child birth as well as envision a positive and happy future for us. There is so much power in our thoughts and in our mind. I was astounded at how the EMD and visualization techniques helped me with the surgery. That was one of the most frightening experiences of my life, but when it came to it I felt an incredible amount of serenity and support from the Spirit. I want to carry that experience through the rest of my life. I can do all things through Christ which strengthened me! I know that and I believe it. I need to cling to it as much now as I did then.

Here is my plan for these last few days as I prepare to bring this child into the world:

1. Spend 5-15 minutes each morning in quiet reflection, imagining who I want to be and how I want to conduct myself in all situations of life. Fill my mind with happy moments from the past and use those positive feelings to project calm and success upon that day and the future.

2. Read aloud my primary purpose twice daily at morning and night.

3. Stop whenever I feel anxiety, frustration, or any kind of negativity, and try to go somewhere quiet and take a moment to re-center myself until I feel faith and calm.

4. Pray frequently and in all situations and states of mind.

5. Write down 3-5 things I'm grateful for each night.

6. Spend 15-30 minutes doing birth relaxation and visualizations.

I really want to have a beautiful, calm, and relaxed birth experience for me and my daughter. I don't want to allow any built-up anxieties or worries about what will happen after she's born to taint that special moment or make me more tense in labor and delivery. I want to feel centered, focused inward upon me and my baby, and in control of myself, and have confidence in my ability to relax and do what my body was designed to do. I've had this kind of experience before with Morgen's birth, and it's what I want to have now with this baby.

Part Four
Miracles

Sunday, December 21, 2014

My heart is full of gratitude today for all the amazing people who have loved and supported us so much this past year. Thank you to all the amazing people who put on the benefit concert, helped watch our kids, helped us out with medical costs, cleaned my house, sent letters and love, and so much more! I have learned how truly good people are. I am grateful to be welcoming our sweet baby girl soon! Merry Christmas to you all!

Tuesday, January 6, 2015

Kiery has arrived! She was born early this morning at 12:16 a.m. after a short, two-hour labor. She's 8 lbs. 6 oz. and is doing great. Because I tested positive for influenza, she has to stay in the nursery, and I have to be in isolation until noon tomorrow. I'm very eager to hold her and see her but am so grateful she came to us whole and healthy. I'm grateful to everyone for their love and prayers! We named her after my good friend, who is one of the strongest, most beautiful and kind people I know. We are so happy and blessed to have our daughter with us!

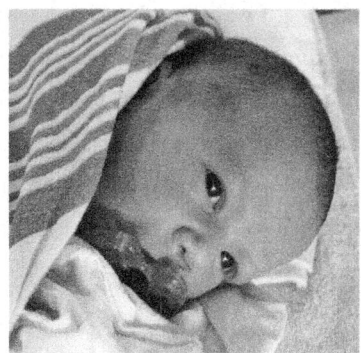

Kiery's Birth Story

Wednesday, January 7, 2015

I'm sitting alone in the hospital room waiting for the moment when the nurse will bring my baby back to me. I haven't seen her or held her for thirty-five hours. I've been counting down every minute. Only three hours left to go. My thoughts have been with her constantly, wondering how she is, if she's crying, and if she knows how much I love her. The staff says she's been doing well, but there's nothing like knowing that for myself. I firmly believe newborns need their mother more than anyone, so the separation has been difficult, but I know it's best for her. Like Ben said last night, "It's the right thing to do, but that doesn't mean it's easy." I laughed and said, "That sounds like the theme of this year." He agreed.

So, that is why I'm sitting here alone and my precious daughter is in isolation in the nursery. Last week, Ben got sick from Micah, and one by one all the kids got it. They had high fevers, terrible coughs, and runny noses, and were very lethargic and run-down. I took care of the family all week, which involved late nights, little sleep, and constant tending. Then on Saturday night, I started feeling ill. By Sunday morning, I was completely sick with one of the most intense illnesses I've ever experienced. Sunday night I ran a fever of 100 to 103 degrees that did not respond much to Tylenol. I called the midwife, and she told me to come in the next morning to evaluate me and the baby. Well, I woke up on Monday and my fever had broken, but I started bleeding. I also had several strong contractions. We rushed to get a good friend to watch the kids for us and went to the hospital.

The nurses immediately got the baby on the monitor and then swabbed me to test for influenza. I continued to have strong but irregular contractions. The results came back from the swab ... I tested positive. They got me on Tamiflu and sent in a prescription for Ben and all of the children. They explained we would have to be on the medication for 48 hours before being considered not contagious. I took the first dose at about 11:30 a.m.

They continued to monitor the baby for several hours. We could have been discharged earlier, but they weren't seeing the fluctuations in her heartbeat that they wanted to see to show that she was really thriving. This continued late into the afternoon, and they became more concerned about her. They ordered an ultrasound to get a better idea of how she was doing. It was a thirty-minute test where they measured different things to see her vitality. She got six out of eight points and so failed the test. The midwife came in and explained that at this point, they would typically induce me and deliver the baby, but because I was still contagious with influenza, they didn't want to risk it. Our goal was to try to hold off delivery for the 48 hours. She said I should come in on Wednesday and be induced at that point if she still wasn't doing well.

So, we went home after a long day in the hospital, eager to see our children and get some rest. We thanked our friend who had watched the kids all day for us, and then Ben took care of the kids while I went to lie down and rest, as I was still having occasional strong contractions. I lay down just after nine, and it felt so good to finally rest in my own bed. I had fallen asleep for no more than ten minutes when I woke up with a really strong contraction. I noted the time and went back to sleep. Six minutes later, I was awakened again. This continued for about thirty minutes. The contractions came closer and stronger, but I tried to relax and keep labor at bay. Ben lay down after cleaning the kitchen and taking care of Naomi, who had woken up still really sick. He'd almost fallen asleep when I knew there was no way we could stall this labor. I told him we needed to go to the hospital, even though I was reluctant to make that decision. I didn't want to go all the way back there only to find out it wasn't real labor. I told him, "I so just want to go to bed and get some rest." But another contraction later, I knew there was no other option. This baby was coming. I felt completely drained from being so sick, having had little rest and a full day in the hospital when I lay down, but something amazing happened. I felt an incredible reserve of strength and energy I cannot account for. I know the Lord blessed me. I felt His Spirit and His calm and knew that though this was the exact time we didn't want her to come, it was going to be okay. This was in His hands, and she was coming at the right time for her.

Ben called his brother and asked him to come over and watch the kids for us. We packed, and I did my deep breathing to get through the powerful contractions. Micah showed up and we left, hoping our still-sick kids would be okay through the night. The car ride was difficult. I never like being confined to a seat during labor. Ben put on his blinkers and floored it. I didn't mind. I knew she was coming quickly.

When we got to the hospital, the nurse wanted to put us back on the monitor. I agreed, as long as I could get into the birthing tub as soon as possible. I knelt in tabletop position on the bed while they monitored the baby. They checked me and I was already 6-7 centimeters dilated. The nurse wasn't happy with the baby's heartbeat again. She wanted to keep me on the monitor, but I was in hard labor and I wanted in the water! She said it was important to stay on the monitor so they would know if baby needed to come sooner. I told her, "Well, if you want the baby to come sooner, let me get in the tub. I'll relax and she'll come faster." She was still resistant, but told me, "I can't stop you if you're going to." I told Ben to go fill up the tub, and despite the nurse's wishes, I got off the monitor and into the tub. The water felt so good and relaxing.

The midwife came in and told me she really would prefer I get back on the monitor so they would know how she was doing. I let her finish her spiel and as soon as she was done, I told her, "I feel pushy." But I wanted her to check me. She said with some surprise, "You're fully dilated. You can push when you feel like doing so." It didn't surprise me. I breathed through another contraction, and then had her break the water. As Ben was helping me get back on all fours, I felt an incredible urge to push. Her head crowned and one push later, she was born right into Ben's hands. He and the midwife brought the baby up out of the water and onto my chest. She immediately began crying as I held her close to me. They got a mask on me and I got to hold my little Kiery for about ten minutes. She had a full head of dark hair, a round face with chubby cheeks, and a double chin. She opened her eyes and blinked up at me. Her body was perfectly whole and healthy. She was beautiful. It was one of the sweetest, most breathtaking moments of my life. There really are no words for that kind of emotion, joy, and spirit. Ben said, "Every time you deliver, the Spirit is so strong." I felt that heaven was near.

I carried her out of the tub, and we went back to the bed with warm blankets for both of us. After the placenta was delivered, the midwife allowed Ben to cut the cord. Then they took Kiery and weighed and measured her. She was 8 lbs. 6 oz. and 19 inches. They wrapped her up, and then the nurse let me take one last look so I could say goodbye before they took her to the nursery. Ben and I haven't seen or held her since. The nurses took pictures with our phones of her first bath and then again last night as she slept in the nursery so we could see how she was doing. Tears are streaming down my face right now. I love her. I miss her. I am grateful she is here. I am grateful the Lord has blessed and sustained both of us through this journey. She is whole. She is healthy. It goes without saying she is living proof a baby can be born normal and healthy while their mother is being treated for cancer. I bore her despite the difficulty of everything we've gone through. I imagined her coming into this world and immediately being with me, but I guess there is yet another challenge we have to surmount. But we're almost there now, and she will very soon be in my arms. She is mine forever.

She is worth every sacrifice. She is my child. The Lord gave her to me and blessed me to be her mother. That is a joy and a responsibility I will forever cherish and strive to fulfill to the upmost degree. Motherhood is sacred. I am grateful and humbled to be so blessed to have precious Kiery as my daughter.

She is strong and sweet and good. I am excited to see what things the Lord and life have in store for our future.

Thursday, January 8, 2015

I'm holding Kiery now and loving every minute of it! We will probably go home tonight or tomorrow morning.

Friday, January 9, 2015

Happily home! We're so grateful to be home, on the mend, and together again! We're so grateful to everyone who watched the kids, cleaned, and brought food. There truly are angels on Earth.

Tuesday, January 13, 2015

Surgery today! I'm grateful for everyone's prayers. These past two weeks have been crazy, but I've felt the Lord's hand so strongly. It's amazing. I'm so grateful to all the people helping us and sending us so much positive energy!

Tuesday, January 20, 2015

Quiet afternoon at home. I can hold her now! Recovery from surgery was rough because they cut through muscle and I can't lift more than five pounds for two weeks. I have a new respect for those who have surgery now! But the doctor gave me the all clear to hold her with my right arm and I'm loving it!

Friday, January 23, 2015

The Hardest and Best Two Weeks of My Life

I'm holding sweet baby Kiery on my lap. She just finished nursing and is now sleeping peacefully. I cherish these quiet moments together. She is a miracle and I treasure her.

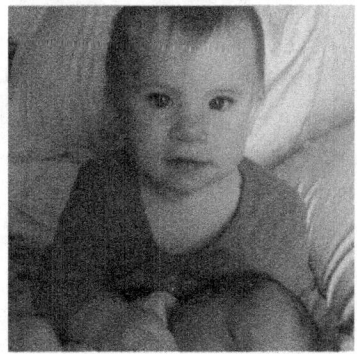

What a whirlwind these past two weeks have been! So much joy, but a lot of trials and blessings as well. We brought Kiery home January 8th and were so happy to have her. The kids and I had to wear masks that first day, but thankfully, she didn't get sick. Ben brought all the kids to the doctor's the next day after he was diagnosed with a sinus and double ear infection due to the flu. The doctor told him there was a 50/50 chance of developing an ear or upper respiratory infection after the flu. Four of the kids had ear infections or chest infections, so they got started on antibiotics. Ben was amazing! He got up with the kids at night and made sure they got their medicine.

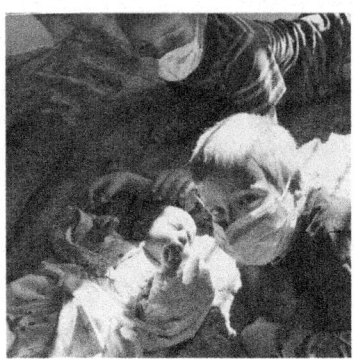

Kiery has been the easiest, sweetest baby. She is so easy to soothe. For the first time ever, we don't find ourselves toting her about the house for hours on end at all hours of the night. She sleeps six to eight hours every night, and that has been such a blessing!

I faced one of the greatest challenges so far when I went in for surgery just a week after giving birth to her. I was told it would be a similar recovery to the mastectomy and wasn't that worried about it, especially since Kiery would not be affected in the womb by it. Boy, was I wrong! It was some of the most intense pain of my life!

The reason why we had to do surgery just one week after Kiery was born was because we only have a small window of time before chemo and radiation start. This surgery is the first step in reconstruction. It's a tissue expander that takes 12 weeks to expand the tissue of my chest to prepare it for the implant. We have to do it now to get the 12 weeks in before radiation, because radiation would damage the skin too much, causing it to lose elasticity and making reconstruction much more difficult. So I went in on Tuesday for surgery. My mom came in from LA and watched the kids for us. Ben had Kiery the whole time.

That first 24 hours, I was in such intense pain, I could not stand up or sit down without tears running down my face. My mom and Ben were my angels through it all, and I could not have done it without them. My mom took care of the five kids, feeding them, dressing them, playing with them, and getting up with them multiple times during the night. Ben took care of Kiery 100%. I couldn't nurse her because of the anesthesia and medications or hold her at all. That night, I slept on the couch, propped up with pillows. Ben spent most of the night up with the baby, while my mom spent many hours up with the kids. Ben not only took care of our newborn, he took care of me too. I couldn't sit up without his help, or go to the bathroom, or bathe, or even wipe my own nose. He had two completely helpless people dependent upon him. And he did it all cheerfully and never once complained. I leaned on him more than I ever had, and he supported me the entire time. He even made me feel beautiful and made me laugh, which only brought on more tears, but it was worth it!

The next three days passed in a similar manner. The pain slowly became more manageable, and I was able to move more. My mom was a superhero and took the kids out to play in the snow and even did homeschooling with them. They had a blast with her. I was so grateful she was there. I was finally able to nurse again, but I still couldn't lift Kiery, so Ben got up faithfully and brought her to me, and then would lay her back down in the bassinette when I was finished.

We went in for my checkup with the surgeon on Monday, and he gave me the go-ahead to lift with my right arm only, so now I can pick her up and do some tasks around the house. I still won't be able to lift with my left arm until Tuesday.

Here's what we're looking at now with my treatment:

On Sunday, we drive up to Denver for my appointments at the University
of Colorado Medical Center on Monday. I go at six a.m. for radiology
appointments. They're going to do a full body scan so they can determine
if there is cancer present anywhere in my body. We'll meet with Dr. Borges
after that and discuss our treatment plan. As it stands right now, chemo will
start mid-February. We'll do a 12-week round followed by radiation and anti-
hormone therapy. Radiation will be every day for six weeks. Anti-hormone
therapy will last a year. After radiation, we'll do a biological chemo for a year.
That chemo is supposed to have minimal side effects but really increases
remission rates.

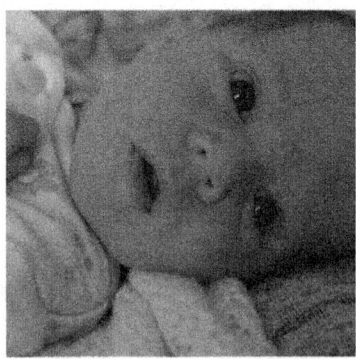

It's a lot to take in, but I feel like after these two weeks, we can take on anything. Childbirth with the flu? Done. 48 hours without my newborn? Done. Surgery one week after childbirth? Done. But I know I couldn't have done any of it without my amazing husband, my angel of a mom, and the Lord who strengthens me and helps me beyond my own capabilities. My faith is strengthened as I witness His hand in our lives, and I know we will be able to meet all challenges as long as we turn to him.

Monday, January 26, 2015

Contrast during a CT scan is one wild experience. Now for a 45 minute nap during the bone scan.

Later that day…

The scans came back clean! There is no cancer in my body! We are thrilled and so grateful. Tears came to my eyes when Dr. Borges told us. The kids are excited too. We still have a year of treatment ahead of us, but tonight, we're celebrating!

Wednesday, February 18, 2015

Started my first chemo treatment for this next 12-week round today. We woke up early and rushed to get the kids off to a friend's house for the day. I cried as I nursed Kiery for the last time. I'm going to miss that closeness and will give her extra snuggles to keep that special bond. It doesn't feel fair to either of us. But then they say life isn't fair. She's been through so much, more than any infant should have, and she's borne it all so well.

For Kiery

You rest in my arms, a milk-drugged smile on your face,

Content, safe and warm.
You're here,
Healthy, hairy and happy,
And I haven't been able to write this for weeks
Because there are no words
For the joy, the bond, the sacredness of your life
And the joy you bring to my life.

I adore your tiny hands, your kissable chubby cheeks
And how you have your father's toes.

I love your coos and the birth of your smiles.
I even love your cries.
They are a siren of your strength and arrival.

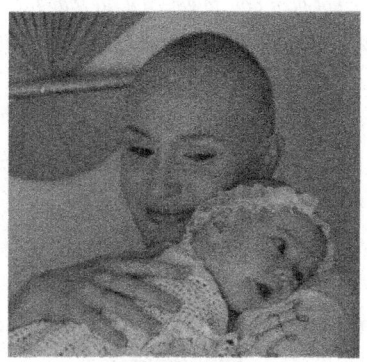

I am awed by your gentle soul
And the magnitude of the spirit that you exude.
In your presence,
I feel I am among the divine.
The greatest title life could give me
In this world of praise and accolades
Is the honor of being your mother.

The bond we share is sacred and eternal.
It's a tie that will not end.
With each other we have everything,
Responsibility, love and an unconditional friend.

I have not been able to give you all that I wanted
And the road before us is still fraught with challenges.
The scariest moment of my life
Was putting you onto the waters
Knowing your fate and mine were not in my hands.
I would sacrifice everything for you,
But I couldn't fix this.
Faith bobbed like a current,
Threatening to be overcome by powerful seas,
But I trusted.
I turned my life and yours
To the one who walked on Galilean waters.
Not my will be done,
But Yours.

Kiery, he held you then.
He holds you now
And He always will.
Trust in the One whose palms
Have your name engraved.
Like me, He loves you more than you know.
He is there with hands outstretched to you
And to every one of us.
The way is always open and never shut.
He is the forgiver of sins,
The purifier of souls.
In His light you will find peace.
When the storms come
And the winds rage and roar,
In Him, you will find refuge.
I know this is true
With every fiber inside of me,
The journey before you won't be easy.
There will be moments when everything comes crashing down,

And you barely have strength to get to your knees,
And you cry out a desperate plea
That there is divine purpose you do not see.
My hope for you in that moment is that you have faith,
Even if you can only hope to believe,
Because I can promise you
That when you seek Him,
You will find.

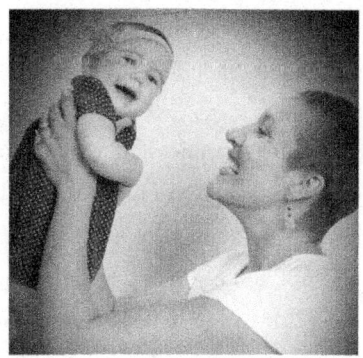

Getting chemo today while holding Kiery. People have asked why I still have to do treatment for a year if the scans came back clean. The scans only detect tumors once they've grown to a point we don't want. So there may be microscopic cells we can't see, and this will get them. Doing this treatment plan increases the survivability rate from 40% to 92%. It's no fun, but we feel like we need to do it.

Saturday, February 21, 2015

Chemo is kicking my trash- so I'm fighting back!

Snuggled under a blanket with Kiery listening to Michael Buble. I've spent most of the past two days this way. It may not look like it, but this is me fighting. Chemo sucks. Period. I sleep 14 hours a day and that doesn't seem enough (poor Ben!). When I'm up, my head is foggy, my stomach is nauseous, and my body tingles all over from the chemo attacking my nervous system. I thought I'd feel better by now. It's been three days since the infusion after all, but I don't. I'm at the point of breaking down. I don't want to do this anymore, and I have so long still to go. Letting it overwhelm me would be easy.

I've learned it's okay to cry. It's okay to admit I'm weak, because that in itself is a strength. But I'm also going to fight back. I'm going to see that there's a purpose in my suffering, even if it's only to entertain my clouded brain for a while, but maybe I can help someone else by sharing my story.

It may be cheesy, but I made this graphic of one of my favorite quotes from Henry Ford to help lift my spirits today, and maybe it will lift others as well. I am determined to work out six days a week even while recovering from the chemo. While on the treadmill, these words keep running through my mind, "I think I can, and I'm right." It would have been easy to say, "I'm too weak. I'm too sick. This hurts too much. It's too hard." And I would have been right. I wouldn't have done it. But I told myself another story. "I am strong. I can do this." And so I did. Watch the stories you tell yourself. If you don't like the plot, change it.

Sending love, health and happiness your way.

Thursday, February 26, 2015

I am so filled with peace and a motivation to change that I cannot sleep despite the nausea and effects of the chemotherapy. Today is the first day of the rest of my life. It is a precious gift, and I'm not going to waste it. Yesterday, I held the hand of my dying friend Mary. The Spirit and a deep sense of love and peace were so strong you could literally feel it vibrating in the air. Holding her hand

and feeling that love, acceptance, and eternity of her soul was one of the most beautiful moments of my life. Mary is a magnificent soul. She has lived a life of trial and hardship, but she has lived it with faith, diligence and charity.

I was struck so deeply by the beauty of a well-lived life. Here was a woman who was not afraid to face death, who was not plagued with regret over standing before her eternal Creator. Her complete serenity inspired me. It has caused me to ask, "How do I want to feel on my deathbed? What do I want to leave behind? How do I want to feel? As I know I too will soon return to my God and Savior." I am determining in this very moment to live so I too may have that peace. So I too will know my Savior as my redeemer and friend and have a clear conscience before Him. So I will look back on my life and see the pure love I had for my husband, my children, and my brothers and sisters here on this earth.

Death can be beautiful, and witnessing the end of a mortal life carries a very valuable opportunity for us. It gives us the chance to remember we are not immortal. We too will someday find ourselves there. It is guaranteed. It gives us the chance to reflect upon our own lives and our own standing before our Eternal Father. It gives us the ability to recognize the incredible gift of a new day, another chance to breathe, to change, and to become, to start over and move forward. And that is what I am going to do. Today and every day. I will not put off becoming the person I want to be, the person I know will be able to look up into my Savior's face, clean, perfected, and holy. I will be that person today.

Friday, February 27, 2015

Cancer Fighting Juice!

I've made a commitment to drink up this super-nutrient green juice four times a week. It has amazing health benefits, and every ingredient is raw, whole, and shown to help prevent and fight cancer. So, yeah, I need it! I still have to chug it down sometimes, but after drinking it daily this past week, I can feel my body actually craving it! I get an energy boost about 15 minutes after I drink it – something I desperately need during this round of chemo – and my mental clarity improves (I need that all the time: mommy brain!)

Anywho, here's the TASTIEST GREEN CANCER FIGHTING JUICE recipe I use:

- 4 Stalks Kale

- 4 Stalks Celery

- 1 Cucumber (I peel mine)

- 1 Lemon

- 4 Green Apples

Wash all fruits and vegetables, put them through your juicer, and drink up!

Sunday, March 1, 2015

There is so much to be happy for! Happiness is a choice. Happiness is medicine. Choose happiness today.

Wednesday, March 4, 2015

Third treatment and Benadryl is kicking in....goodnight world.

Friday, March 6, 2015

Tough day: vomiting, sick kids, mouth sores, and Ben's working. Don't feel I have much to give, just a positive thought.

Thursday, March 12, 2015

"When you go to your limits, your limits expand."
–Robin Sharma

It's 4 a.m. and despite how exhausted I am, I can't sleep as Taxol rages through my body. Strange tingling sensations shoot up and down my face, neck, and limbs as it attacks my nervous system. I wanted to write down my thoughts while they are so poignant in my mind. These words keep coming to me, "When you go to your limits, your limits expand." I feel like I have come to my limits many times these past nine months, especially in the past nine weeks as I have experienced incredible amounts of pain and fatigue while still tending to the needs of my newborn baby. Either one of those experiences is enough to bring me to my limits. But I have seen how those limits have expanded each time I have reached them.

I heard a quote from a wise person recently that said, "There is no growth in the comfort zone. And there is no comfort in the growth zone." I don't know if that last part is entirely true, because I have felt incredible comfort from my husband, family, friends, and the Lord during this, but what I think they mean is that growth itself is uncomfortable, just like when you're trying to strengthen a muscle. You have to tear the muscle down first before you can make it strong.

I think that's what being a mother is about. It's continuing to give when you feel you have nothing left to give. I remember experiencing that with each of my children. I remember walking around and around our tiny living room and dining room, bouncing Joseph hour after hour into the night, wondering what I was doing wrong and why I couldn't get him to stop crying. I hoped I would at least have strong biceps. I remember feeling like an utter failure as I again bounced another baby, Morgen this time, on our second story landing, looking up at the brilliant stars through the skylight and pleading with the Lord as tears streamed down my face, "Please just let her go to sleep. I have to get some sleep." But she just kept crying. So I kept walking, knowing that in just a few hours, the other children would awaken and I would have to take care of them, sleep or no sleep.

I remember going outside our small duplex home in Provo and sitting on the front porch step sobbing as Chance wailed in the office. My neighbor came home, and I was too spent, too beyond reasoning to feel embarrassed as she put her arm around me and asked what was wrong. "I feel like the worst Mom in the world." I told her. "My baby is in there crying, and I don't know how to help him. I keep trying, but it doesn't make any difference. I don't know what to do."

Just this past week, I found myself at that point again, feeling I had done all I could do, given everything I could, and it wasn't enough. It was two in the morning and Kiery was still fussing. She was sick and congested with her first cold, and I was barely over having the stomach flu. I was also still battling the effects of the chemotherapy. Despite the fact Ben had helped me get more rest than I otherwise would have and the fact that he was the one holding her and not me, I broke down. "Why won't she sleep?" I asked us both. "We need to sleep. I can't do this anymore." But somehow and in some way, I kept going. Because that's what mothers do. We keep going when we feel we can't go anymore, and we never give up. No matter how weak, tired, and inadequate we feel, we keep going.

Friday, March 13, 2015

Yesterday, I was unhappy with my hair because it's such an awkward length. Then last night it started falling out again, and I realized how much I like my hair.

Monday, March 16, 2015

My last day before I shave my head. I don't know how many times I want to fish my hair out of Kiery's mouth! Ben is amazing. Every time I'm too sick for the job, he takes over, which is pretty much all the time.

Friday, March 20, 2015

Back to bald!

Wednesday, March 25, 2015

Chemo makes me cold. But we're halfway there today! Only six more left! We're all going to have to celebrate when this is done!

My amazing husband is taking all six kids, including the new baby, to the discovery museum today. He's so brave!

Wednesday, April 1, 2015

So, if you've ever wondered what it's like to go through chemo, this is for you. Everyone experiences it differently, but this is my experience.

Wednesday: Wake up at 7 a.m. Do quick "Bikini Body Mommy Challenge" workout. Take a shower and rush to get diaper bag prepped and kids ready. Friends (or this week my mom was here) come to watch kids around 9 a.m.

Hurry to the hospital and go into the Cancer Center, and then to the back where the Infusion Center is. It's an open room with about 15 or so chairs in it, with IVs beside each one. The mornings are pretty quiet, which is nice, but we bring Kiery with us, so it's usually not quiet for long. The staff are SO friendly and always ask how we're doing. They access my port (a device put under my skin just beneath my collar bone that has an IV tube that goes directly into the main vein leading from my upper body to my heart; this is the safest and most convenient way to administer chemo) and draw blood. They send the blood to the lab to run my blood cell counts, and to check liver function, iron levels, and so forth. Once they get the go-ahead from the lab techs, they administer pre-meds including steroids, anti-nausea meds, and Benadryl to keep me from having an allergic reaction and minimize initial side effects. The Benadryl makes me super sleepy and hits me in a giant wave, so I'm pretty out of it after that. Then they administer two to three types of chemo, depending on the week. But Ben and I talk, and I snuggle Kiery on my lap, and sometimes we nap together. Ben gets us lunch, but I'm usually too tired to eat. Sometimes I'm nauseous, like today. That's no fun.

Infusion lasts three to five and a half hours, and then we drive back to our home in Bayfield. I usually need a nap by then. I sleep a couple of hours in the afternoon / evening. The Benadryl wears off. My nose drips, and I get bloody noses daily. The drippy nose hasn't stopped for a single day since I've started.

At about seven that night, the Taxol chemotherapy hits my nervous system. It starts on my cheekbones; it is a strange tingling sensation like when your foot falls asleep, only a little stronger, and nothing I do changes it. That tingling sensation then spreads down my arms, legs, and chest. By about 9 p.m., the electric shooting sensations start. They feel like waves of electricity passing through my body. It doesn't hurt, but it is annoying and very difficult to ignore. I take more Benadryl to help me sleep, but it doesn't work. I'm usually up at three or four in the morning. That's why I'm up right now typing this instead of sleeping. No matter how tired I am, it's almost impossible for me to ignore these sensations as they race up and down my body while I'm lying in bed. It's good thinking time, though. Tonight I came up with an idea for my book about an electric river with currents of blue energy passing through it. Thank you, Taxol!

Thursday: I'm pretty tired Thursdays. Ben lets me sleep in after taking care of the baby for me once I do finally fall asleep. The fatigue is pretty amazing. It's like trying to walk through thick fog all day. My mind is cloudy, and my body is just run down. Despite this, I run first thing, about three miles. It's so hard! But I feel like it's important to sweat out the chemo as much as I can, so I can get it out of my system and hopefully feel better faster. Ben does homeschooling with the kids. I help read with them if I can. I take a nap and work on my writing. It's a good distraction.

Friday and Saturday: That's when the chemo hits my vision. My eyesight becomes blurry, and I really shouldn't drive on those days at all. I get the fishbowl effect. The edges of my vision are somewhat distorted and hazy; the perception is frustrating. I call these my brain-dead days. Sometimes it's hard to focus. I also get diarrhea the worst on these days and bad stomach cramps. These are usually my most frustrating days. My energy improves, but never enough to do all the things I want to do. Ben is still amazing at taking care of the kids while trying to get work done on our business and attend church and our callings. It's a lot. I try to take it in stride and remember this won't last forever.

Monday and Tuesday: These are the days Ben and I think we're super humans. We try to cram in a week's worth of work into two days! Ben goes to the shop and to meetings, and works on our businesses. I cram laundry, house cleaning, homeschooling, grocery shopping, meeting with my counselor, and, of course, writing and publishing my books into a few, all-too-short hours. I often wear myself out, because I feel the best I do all week and overdo it. But we have a lot of fun, too, with family home evening, scouts, and time outside together. I make sure to give the kids lots of my "happy" time and attention.

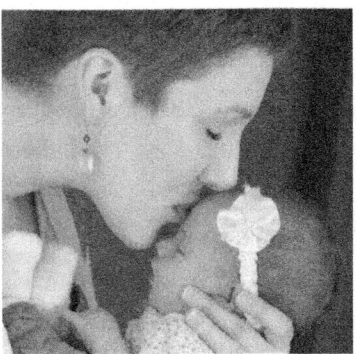

Yay! Treatment seven done. Five more to go. Feeling sick to my stomach but so grateful for wonderful friends and family helping me get through this! Grateful my mom is here, for all the incredible women of our ward, and, of course, for my husband, who serves me unceasingly! Thank you.

Thursday, April 2, 2015

There is a song my dad wrote for me when I was a baby. Now, he dedicates it to me and my baby, Kiery, who fought alongside me while we went through cancer treatment together during my pregnancy. Kiery is three months old now and healthy and well! This song brings tears to my eyes...every time. Thank you, Dad!

Sunday, April 5, 2015

Times are rough. On top of dealing with chemo, Ben and I have hit financial rock-bottom. The stress and strain of that is almost more than we can bear. It has been particularly difficult for Ben, as he feels pulled between having to take care of me and the kids while also trying to provide for us. He isn't sure what it is he should be doing right now, and we both feel trapped. For most of this year, our auto body business has been able to provide for us even as Ben has stepped away to take care of me. We also got through a lot of it due to the generous donations from crowdfunding. Both of these have been such a blessing.

But this winter was really dry, and the entire auto body business in this area is not doing well. Gas prices went down, which has hurt our local economy, because our biggest industries are oil and gas. So people are scared and hurting here, and they're holding onto their money and choosing not to repair their damaged vehicles. Ben has done a phenomenal job running our business the past five years, but now we're looking at potentially going out of business, partly due to the economy and partly due to the fact that I have been Ben's biggest priority this year.

I can't help but feel guilty. I didn't ask for cancer. I didn't ask for chemotherapy. I wish we didn't have to go through it, but we did. What else can we do? I'm scared right now. I'm not well. I wish I could say I could just handle it, but this isn't like coming down with the flu for a week. We still have five weeks of chemotherapy to deal with. In the meantime, we can't make payroll, pay our mortgage, or buy groceries without using our credit cards. I'm so grateful we have insurance and have had the help of so many, but I'm scared and confused right now.

Ben is not doing well. He's stressed and I have never seen him so scared and weak. He is not weak. He has borne all of this with such strength, compassion and faith. But he's really struggling right now. He feels like a failure when all he's tried to do is help and support me. What else was he supposed to have done? It feels like we're being punished because we chose to be unified as we faced this. Perhaps my perceptions are all wrong right now. Perhaps this is one of those journal entries I'll look back on and want to delete, but I don't think I should delete it. It's real. It's raw. It's what we're going through. And it is one of the most difficult things we've had to face. The challenges of me having cancer are so much more than just physical. It has affected every aspect of our lives. The strain on financial and familial relationships on top of everything else is breaking us down right now. It feels like too much to bear. I'm trying to be positive, but all my positivity doesn't bring money into our bank account.

The children will be up soon. How are we going to do this? I don't think there is anything I could have done differently. I just wish we weren't in this situation. I wish there were a clear answer. I'm begging for a reprieve.

One thing we often say is, "It will work out. We're going to live through this." And that's true. We will. But boy, is it hard.

Wednesday, April 8, 2015

I've been criticized for having a "Pollyanna" attitude. If that's the worst thing you can say about me, I must be doing pretty good! I have to watch my thoughts constantly. I haven't always been the most positive person, but I've learned it's best!

Kiery was my comfort and snuggle buddy today.

Saturday, April 11, 2015

I just read a post on Facebook from one of my cancer friends. Her cancer was in remission, the scans came back clean. Now they just did an MRI and found cancer all in her spine. She is angry and scared. They're giving her weeks, maybe a few months, to live. She doesn't want to leave her two kids. It breaks my heart. There will always be that part of me that will wonder if this will happen to me. Will the cancer come back? Will I be told I have weeks to live?

I'm so sad for her, and I'm rattled by this. Once again, I face the fact that at any time, life could be over. I have no control over it. I realize I've fallen once again into the illusion that I know what's going on in my life. I've told myself this is almost all over. I'm nearing the end of the most intense part of treatment. I'll finish out the year, and it will be over. Cancer will be gone. I'll move on with the rest of my life. That's how I want it to be, but I don't *know* if that's how it will be. All I can do is make the best of the time that is given me.

Sunday, April 12, 2015

We blessed sweet Kiery Celeste today. So grateful to Heavenly Father for her!

Wednesday, April 15, 2015

Getting treatment nine right now. The fatigue is compounding every week. I don't want to do this anymore.

Monday, April 20, 2015

I don't think there are words to describe how difficult this is or how scared I am. I have three treatments left, five more weeks of feeling sick. I know I'm nearing the end of this. Everyone seems to think it's already over: the baby is here, the scans came back clean, the most intense chemo is almost done, and life will soon return to normal. They have no idea how much I'm struggling right now to get through each hour, let alone each day. The effects of the chemo are compounding. I'm so tired, and no matter how much I sleep, I can't take the edge off the fatigue that is my constant companion. My hands are numb and weak most of the time. I can barely type these words right now. I dropped the bottle three times this morning trying to feed Kiery. I have to use a pillow or my knee to keep my hand supported. But none of that is the most frightening part to me.

I don't want to be over-dramatic, but I am really afraid. I can literally feel my body breaking down and weakening. For the first time in this whole year, I feel like I am dying. Not like I'm going to die tomorrow, but as if I know in some primal part of me that this chemo will eventually kill me. Modern medicine has proven that much in the laboratory. Many types of chemo are lethal if administered in certain doses. That's what chemo does. It's designed to kill cells, targeting rapidly dividing cells. But this isn't some logical understanding I'm talking about. It's a physical knowledge that my body is weakening. I can feel the chemo killing my good cells. I'm weaker now than I have ever been in my life.

The chemo is also affecting my mental capacities. It's as if I've been struggling to keep my face above water, but this week I finally submerged. Wednesday, Thursday, Friday, and most of Saturday, my mind was muddled. My thoughts were unfocused, and it was difficult to understand what was going on or interact with the external world. It was terrifying, and very often frustrating. I told Ben it was like being five or six inches underwater, watching the world above and trying to understand it, but all the noises are distorted and the images are contorted.

I was working on one of my books and a few files to send to my virtual assistants, but I couldn't find them again a few hours later. I didn't know where I'd saved them, because they weren't in the folder I remembered saving them to or in any other that would make sense. I know I worked on it for several hours, but even now, I can't find any evidence of it. I can't remember conversations I had the same day, and on Friday, I couldn't remember which child had done their reading with me and which one hadn't.

On Friday, I woke up at two in the morning when Kiery cried, and I couldn't go back to sleep. When I'm up for hours in the middle of the night, I usually pull out my tablet, curl up on the couch, and get some work done on my writing and publishing. But I knew that if I did that, I wouldn't be able to focus. I couldn't remember what I needed to do or who I needed to contact, or what I should write about. It was like trying to grab at a plastic bag tossing in the wind. Every time I reached for it, it would fly away. I knew what I should be able to do and think, but I just couldn't do it. I couldn't take advantage of my nightly wakefulness, I curled myself against Ben and realized I was trembling. What if I always felt like this? What if my mind never cleared? What if the "chemo brain" became permanent? That thought still scares me.

The experience I had this week gave me a real appreciation for those who have mental limitations. My heart goes out to them, and I feel like I understand in some small way how very challenging it is. I have much more compassion for them now.

Finally, on Saturday afternoon, I felt like I had finally broken through the surface of confusion and had my mental clarity back. I told Ben, "I can think right! My thoughts are clear. I can focus!" But the fog returned that evening. It's been on and off since then. Today (Monday), I feel pretty good. I'm still tired, but I feel like my mind is my own again. I go in again on Wednesday. I have to have three more doses of the poison that is weakening my body and clouding my mind. My only consolation is that if it is hurting me this badly, it must really be wreaking havoc on any cancer cells still present in my body. So, do I trade three weeks of misery for a lifetime of health? Reason tells me yes. But everything else screams at me, "No! I can't take any more. I don't want to do it."

Sigh. But I have to. I've come so far. I can't quit now, right? But I want to. I so want to.

I feel awful physically, but I'm working overtime on being positive and recognizing the incredible blessings in my life. As I look at sweet Kiery smiling at me in Ben's arms, see his encouraging smile, and laugh as Naomi squeals at the fish by my chair, I know how much the Lord has blessed me. And I am so grateful for all the earthly angels that help make this much easier on us!

Thursday, April 30, 2015, 5:00 a.m.
(Again, the day after chemo, and I can't sleep from the Taxol affecting my nerves.)

This is awful. Can I just say that? I am fighting my way out of hell, inch by inch, desperate to get my life back, desperate to get my head above the water that surrounds me enough to take a breath, to think clearly, to actually be me again. I want so badly to help Ben, but I've had to surrender to the fact that I just can't. Not now. Not for a few more weeks. But soon. I must find peace in that. I must know that it is okay. Last week, there was a day I fed the baby only once. Once in 24 hrs. That shows how much more Ben has taken on. Serving me, our new baby, and our five other children 'round the clock – meals; laundry; homeschool; keeping the house clean. Even as the pressures of our business and financial needs mount upon him. We were laughing last night about how dire our needs are when there is something that comes before our basic financial needs. But that's how it is right now.

We've had three months of no income other than generous donations and help from others. This hasn't been comfortable or easy for us, although we are grateful. Ben takes his role as provider for us very seriously, and he's had to set that aside for the time being. He is incredible. He has never once complained. Once again, I feel completely supported by him. He is truly keeping his vows: in sickness and in health. I am so incredibly grateful for him.

I need him now more than ever. This treatment is nearing its end, but this battle is far from over. Nearly everything in me wants to quit right now. I'm physically and emotionally drained. These last weeks have been the hardest part of this whole year for me. I feel as if I keep getting buffeted by waves that don't end. And they've finally submerged me. I have nothing left to give. I sleep 14-16 hours a day and mostly lie on the couch the rest of the time. I'm just too weak. When I try to do more, my head is fuzzy and I can't think right. I had the baby for a few hours Monday while Ben went to the shop to get some much needed work done. She started crying, and I couldn't remember the last time I had fed her. Had it been 30 minutes? Two hours? I literally couldn't remember, and trying to only made me more confused. My hands shake and are so weak that I nearly dropped the baby last week. We were at a friend's house one day, and I reached out to hand the baby to Ben, when my wrists gave out. Luckily, he was right there to catch her. Just like he always is. But it was shocking to me. I had underestimated just how weak I had become. I've had to be much more careful since then, using my elbows, knees, and lap to support her. I tried to write in my journal last night, but my fingers couldn't hold the pencil well enough to jot down even a few scratchy lines.

I want so badly to quit. I don't think anyone knows how much I want to. But there's a small seed in me that says, "It's not enough to be a good starter. You have to be a good finisher as well." I've started this. I will finish it. I have it to do and so I will do it. It's sheer grit at this point and the strength the Lord gives me that I feel I don't deserve but still plead for and receive.

My head broke through the surface just long enough this morning for me to think of a few lines about a mother's hands. My neuropathy from the chemo has made me notice and appreciate my hands more than ever.

A Mother's Hands

I wake up, kneel beside my bed
Hands fold in prayer,
Tiny hands touch my back before my "amen" is said,
Gentle voice asking for breakfast.
I push myself up, give her a hug,
Hands shaking slightly as I open a bag of cereal,
Get a bowl, pour the milk.

Next, I lift a little one, wipe sleepy tears from her eyes,
Change a diaper and her clothes.
More cereal.
Soon I'm mopping up spilled milk
And chasing runaway Cheerios.
My hands gather books as I try to answer questions.
They stop a fight, put a child into time-out.
They get down boxes of toys and turn on Elmo.
Another fight, more tears wiped away.
There isn't time to fold them for prayer,
But I offer one anyway.

My hands brush hair, she wants an "Elsa" braid,
Put on shoes, feet racing out the door.
Minutes later, they put on a Band-Aid
After soothing with a hug.
My hands spread peanut butter, chop apples.

Next, they're washing peanut butter and jelly out of a toddler's hair,
Bubbles and giggles,
Then laying her down for nap time.
Bottles are made and my hands tremble as I shake the bottle.
When did my hands become so weak?
None of these tasks are new to me. I never really noticed I did them before,
But now, I do.

My hands don't have the strength to hold my baby,
So I have to press her against me to keep her safe.
I rock her until she falls asleep.
I kneel beside my husband at our bed,
Our hands clasp in prayer.
He doesn't know I can barely feel his,
But it doesn't matter, I know they're there.
We each offer up our silent prayer,
And I thank my Heavenly Father for my hands.
They serve me so often and so well.
I hope they serve Him too.
And I thank him for my mother's hands,
Countless years she served and sacrificed.
Her hands blessed, nurtured and healed.
And all that time I never knew just how much she did,
But now I do.

My mind thinks of another pair of hands as well,
The hands that belonged to His Son,
Those perfect hands that healed the sick,
Comforted the downtrodden,
Broke and blessed bread,
Those hands that never once were raised in anger,
That never pointed the finger of scorn,
That never hurt or accused another,
That my burdens and sins were borne.

His beautiful hands, pierced by cruel and painful nails,
Bleeding as He hung by them upon the cross,
Hands of mercy and purest love
Sacrificed for me.
My name engraved upon the palms.

Even now, I can see His hands,
Stretched forth and reaching for me.
"Your hands give much," He whispers,
"But I have given all. Rest your burdens and sins upon me,
And I will carry, even thee."

Friday, May 15, 2015

I'm sitting here getting Herceptin at the infusion center. It's been a week since my last chemo treatment. I keep waiting to feel better, but it hasn't happened yet. I'm optimistic I will start feeling better soon, though. Man, it's been rough, but at least that part is behind us. It can only get better from here. I've really been focusing on my nutrition and making sure I'm getting lots of antioxidants to boost my immune system and kick this nasty cough and cold. I'm planning to do a juice and raw food detox with my aunt starting on Sunday. I hope this will help flush out any remaining chemo, clean out my gut, improve my metal clarity, and help me lose some weight. I plan to lose 20 pounds over the next few months. It should be easier now that I'm not taking steroids with the chemo, which will increase my energy levels.

We're looking to move next week as well. There's just not much more we can do here with the shop, and we need income. Ben's looking at going back to flight school as well. Flying is what he really loves, but it will be hard for me with him gone so much. Facing all these changes and decisions while not feeling well and not having my full mental clarity has been difficult. I'm really trying to focus on faith and not fear. But it's hard, so hard. I feel flattened, pressed thin. You can see right through me, and I can't even think about it.

Thursday, May 21, 2015

I was too sick and busy these past days to write at all. We are in the middle of moving, and my mind can't even focus. I am grateful to the angel friends we have and to my sister Jasmine, who came to help us pack and clean. I can't do it. I know I should be able to, but every time I try – there is nothing there. I can barely think at all. I just focus on breathing and moving. And in the midst of it all, we have to rush and clean up the house to show it to prospective buyers. I've never felt so physically weak. I can't be mom. I can't do anything. I don't want anyone to experience this. Ever.

Saturday, May 23, 2015

We have moved to Yoder, Colorado, which is a remote country town east of Colorado Springs. It is flat like paper, brown and boring, and it reminds me of how I feel, but at least we're together and with family.

I am exhausted but relieved to be here and so grateful to be done showing the house. That was crazy.

We're living in a camper on Ben's parents' land. Things are not great for us financially, and until our house sells and Ben gets a job here, we won't be able to get a place of our own. Ben's pretty down on himself about it, but I'm optimistic – it's just another step towards our fabulous future.

Sunday, May 31, 2015

I've actually been really happy since we moved here. I dreaded moving into a camper and thought it would be horrible, but it actually hasn't been too bad. It's crowded for sure, with six kids, a dog, and a cat in that tiny thing, but we've made it work. I'm just so relieved not to be packing and showing the house anymore.

My physical energy and strength are improving as well, and I'm noticing a real difference. I've started running three times a week, pushing the three girls three miles in the double running stroller on the bumpy dirt roads out here, and it makes me feel so good!

Ben has been working like mad to get us situated and comfortable here. He's also looking for a job while we sell our house and business back in Bayfield. I'm struggling to find ways to buoy him up. He feels like a failure because the business isn't doing well and wasn't able to support us these past three months. I know he's done the best he could. I needed him, and he was there for me. It is unfortunate what has happened to the business, but so much of it was out of his control. I don't want him to blame himself.

"Whatever the mind can Conceive and Believe..."
—Napoleon Hill

Part Five
Changes

Sunday, June 14, 2015

I learned today that radiation will permanently damage 10-15% of my left lung. How crazy is that? I'm having a hard time wrapping my mind around it. The radiation oncologist explained how one of the beams used in my treatment will hit that lung, but that because I'm young and healthy I "probably won't notice it at all." I try really hard to take good care of my body. I hate the idea that radiation will permanently damage a healthy organ.

The radiation oncologist explained that we will use a "breath hold" technique during the treatment. The idea is to move the heart back a centimeter by taking in a deep breath and holding it. He said, "The lungs are kind of like the kidneys. You can live just fine without one. But you only have one heart."

I'm going in tomorrow to do a practice run to make sure I'm taking the same kind of breath each time. Kind of freaking out about it all right now....

Monday, June 15, 2015

Dr. Borges wrote me back explaining how important the radiation treatment is for my long-term health. She explained that chemo is kind of like "sweeping and mopping" away any cancer cells that are there. Radiation is like "coming in with bleach and dousing everything to make sure the cancer can never come back."

The side effects should be some fatigue that compounds throughout the weeks and a sunburn-like reaction at the radiation site.

Thursday, June 18, 2015

A year ago today, a doctor looked me in the eye and said, "If you keep your baby, you're risking your life." I'm still here, and so is my baby. I don't hold any grudges against those who opposed my decision, but I'm grateful for my inner conviction and for our Heavenly Father who guided us through those difficult times and decisions. So, today is like my second birthday, because every year I'm here is one I'm grateful for.

Saturday, June 20, 2015

Ben got a job! That's a huge blessing. He's working at ABRA collision center in Colorado Springs as an estimator.

Week one of radiation is done. I feel fine so far. It's just been frustrating how little I get done. I have to go in every day, Monday through Friday, for the next six and a half weeks. Being out here in the country means it takes a minimum of three hours out of my day! I'm in the middle of trying to launch my new fantasy series and writing the sequel to Swab.

The kids love living here in Yoder, even though we're in a camper. They have so much fun playing with their cousins, riding bikes, swimming in the pool, and dirt biking. I'm grateful for the support from Ben's parents and the rest of our family here.

Ben and I have really been doing a lot of pondering on how we can use this past year to benefit others. There are so many incredible lessons we've learned that could bless many people.

Wednesday, June 24, 2015

I lost 95% of my eyelashes and eyebrows this week. I didn't think THAT was going to happen this long after chemo. Why am I taking it harder than losing my hair? Because even guys have eyelashes and eyebrows. Not looking very feminine right now. And it makes me sad, okay? But there's another thing I get to add to my gratitude list, even if I'm doing it grudgingly.

Wednesday, July 1, 2015

Having to drive two hours every single day, five days a week, for radiation is such a pain. But at least all the people there are really nice, and if I just hang on, it'll be done before I know it. The fatigue is getting worse, but it's nothing like chemo.

I lie on a custom-fitted pad that ensures my upper body, arms, and neck are in the same exact position every time. After the technicians set everything up, they leave the room and speak to me over an intercom. They tell me to take in a breath and then hold it. It's then my job to hold my breath until they tell me to breathe again. Usually it's about 12-15 seconds, so it's not a big deal. The idea is to use a breath hold to expand the lungs and push my heart back a centimeter so it isn't irradiated. It's kind of scary to think about sometimes. I have to be so perfectly still, but I'm confident it will be okay.

Thursday, July 9, 2015

Still living in the camper. That probably won't change for at least another two months, since we have to sell our house and business before we can put in any offer. But I have only EIGHT MORE RADIATION TREATMENTS! Can you tell I'm excited about that?

I'm getting more red and sore, but mostly I'm looking forward to having my days back. I haven't been able to do nearly the amount of writing I would like to, but one good thing is we're catching up on homeschool in the car. (It's not ideal, but I love multitasking!) Another week and a half and we'll be done with the hard stuff.

Saturday, July 11, 2015

My echocardiogram showed that my left ventricle function has been reduced by 15%. My oncologist has therefore postponed my Herceptin treatment for six weeks to see if it will recover. If it doesn't, that means it was damaged by the radiation and that will be permanent. I'm pretty bothered by this news. I've worked hard to exercise regularly and eat healthy to take good care of my heart, so to learn that it is suffering is hard to swallow.

Monday, July 20, 2015

I'm DONE WITH RADIATION! Hallelujah! Maybe I can have a life again?

Monday, July 27, 2015

There are burns in my armpit from radiation. Everything should heal within the next two weeks?

Thursday, September 3, 2015

The anti-hormone medication makes me feel like a crazy woman. I can't stand it. They said to expect "some mood swings," but this is ridiculous. I've been snapping at the kids, and I cry at the drop of a button. I noticed a marked difference in my ability to handle things the day I started it. And this is such a bad time to not be at my best emotionally. Ben's working 60 hours a week, which means I'm on parent duty 24/7, because he doesn't get up with the baby or kids at night. We're trying to get caught up on homeschool. We're living in a camper. I'm publishing one book of the Jonas Flash Chronicles every three weeks. And we're trying to negotiate purchasing a house and getting approved for a loan.

Tuesday, September 8, 2015

I did something naughty. I stopped taking the anti-hormone meds. I just couldn't take it anymore. Physical health is important, but so is mental and emotional health. Dr. Borges probably isn't going to be very happy with me when I see her on Thursday, but I feel so much better this week since I stopped. Being a happy mom and wife is worth it. I've made a decision and am sticking to it.

Friday, September 11, 2015

Had an echocardiogram this week, and it came back good! My left ventricle is back to normal function. That's great news because it means the damage came from the Herceptin and not the radiation, which would have been permanent. So, Dr. Borges wants to start up the Herceptin again. She approved of me stopping the anti-hormone therapy to let my body readjust to normal hormone levels; later I'll start it again at a lower dose. She also prescribed a light antidepressant to help with mood levels. That gave me a lot of hope.

Saturday, September 12, 2015

Kiery and I went to get her baby pictures taken today. The lady doing the pictures heard me call Kiery "my miracle" and asked what that was about, so I told her a little about our story. After hearing it, she insisted I get in and take some pictures with her.

Tonight, when I viewed them, I was surprised at how little I recognized myself. So much has changed this past year. I don't know how my mind has been able to keep up with it all. I wrote this poem tonight to capture the emotions and experience that have accompanied this entire crazy, difficult, but ultimately beautiful journey.

New Reflection
The face that gazes back at me is one I barely recognize.
It's funny, but in my mind's eye,
I still see myself as the person I was before.
I don't realize how much has changed,
But it has.

You can see it as clear as if an artist had painted it.
My face is a bit harder,
The hardness that comes from suffering,
The lines that come from pain,
And the burdens of weakness.
There is more depth to my eyes.
They've looked into depths of fear,
Spent nights wide awake too terrified to blink.
How many times did I question,
Am I going to make it?
Will my baby be all right?
My eyes tell that story now,
Blue as the evening sky that knows the

Darkness of the night.
There is resilience in my chin.
That might sound strange,
But I never saw it there before.

I hold my head differently.
I'm more sure of myself,
More confident in my ability to choose my own way.
There is more joy in my smile.
I used to pose and remember my modeling training
Whenever a camera was on,
But with my loved ones near,
My happiness is real.

There is more warmth in my arms,
A sure strength and devotion
Of pure love and sacrificeFor the little one they cradle
And will love for eternity.
I may not be used to the person staring back at me,
But that's who I am,
Scarred and disfigured,
Weakened and burned,
Sick and struggling,
But growing,
Learning,
Strengthening,
Improving,
Serving,
And striving to be the best me,
All the days of my life.

Epilogue

WHAT I HAVE LEARNED SINCE FIGHTING CANCER WHILE PREGNANT

Fighting cancer while pregnant and as a mom brought so many personal changes for me, all of which were about being better to myself. I am walking into the future knowing more about who I am, what I want, and how I will be of service to others. I take full responsibility for my life and what shows up in it. I understand, more now than ever before, the power of my mind and my emotions at the level of happiness and success in my life. I've learned the importance of being more interested in others than interesting to them. I now know how to be fully present and appreciative of the moment, regardless of what is happening. I can laugh at toddler messes, dance to my favorite song in the carpool lane, and delight in the beautiful imperfection of this incredible life.

WE ARE THE CREATORS OF OUR REALITY

First, we are the creators of our own reality. This is a great thought when things are going well, but not such a good one when they aren't. We don't want to think that we are responsible for the negative things in our experience, but the reverse side is that we always have the power to change them. Our

Heavenly Father has given us these creative powers, and it is our calling to master our own inner powers.

I have come to understand clearly that our thoughts and emotions attract like things into our experience. When we learn to master our mental faculties, and put our emotional and mental energy more upon what we want than what we do not want, we are blessed with more of what we want. What we focus on grows, so I challenge you to think about what you're growing with your thoughts. Flowers or weeds? The Lord said, "For as a man thinketh, so is he." Learning how to master my own mind and emotional state has brought me greater peace, contentment, and success than I ever could have thought possible. I know that it is because when I put my energy into the good of this universe, the good that Heavenly Father has given us, I am allowing myself to receive and experience more of it.

OUR CHALLENGES ARE OPPORTUNITIES TO GROW AND BE REBORN

Being diagnosed with life-threatening cancer at the age of only 29 was one of the greatest gifts I could have been given, because through it, I was reborn. I was given a precious second chance at life. It allowed me to wake up and realize what was truly important, and let go of what was not. I wake up every day now knowing that life is short and precious and that each moment is a gift. I have vowed not to waste it, but to use my time, energy, and talents to help others. In this way, I am experiencing greater joy and peace of mind than I ever knew before.

Challenges continue to come. Life is not "perfect" – and I'm completely, blissfully accepting of that. Because in each challenge that comes lies the seed to become stronger and grew anew into the world, if we allow it.

Just recently, we learned that my husband's pay was to be cut in half from what was originally promised him. We were shocked and yes, scared. It was so far from what we'd expected after having moved our big family of eight fifteen hours to another state. Not fun! But I knew it was an opportunity to grow yet again and that even this difficulty would lead to greater good for us in the end.

I use writing as therapy, and after I did an exercise I call "Slay the Dragon" to get out all the negativity and frustration, I then had the room within me to look at the situation constructively. In a Livestream on Facebook, I shared how we have the opportunity to bring more "water" or "fire" to any situation. Water is anything that is healing, soothing, productive, and forward-moving. Fire is anything that is not. When you complain, lash out in anger at injustices, or hold onto resentment, you're adding more fire to the fire. To change any situation, you must bring more water than fire to it.

I've been criticized for being too "Pollyanna," saying that all you have to do is think positively and everything will work out. I'm not that naive. But I do know that in every situation, we have a choice. We can either buckle and give in to the adversity in life, doubling the suffering and difficulty of it, or we can see the good in it and allow it to bless us. I choose the happier road.

It has saved my life and given me a new one.

Power and Peace Are Always Available to Us

We cannot go so far down into darkness that the light of healing and peace of Christ cannot find us. One of the greatest lies the adversary likes to tell us is that we have gone too far, sinned too greatly to ever be worthy of forgiveness, let alone happiness. We think it may apply to others, but not to us. We are the exception, and there is no hope for us. That is not true. Christ is always there, whether we choose to see him or not. He stands with open arms and hands, ready and willing to receive us. Our names are engraved upon His palms. He knows and loves each one of us. We are precious to Him.

He wants us to be happy.

But it is, and ever will be, our choice.

GRATITUDE

We choose to be happy and accept all of the power and peace available to us by being grateful for what we have. During treatment, I wrote an entire ebook about this titled the "Gratitude Dare," which challenges you to do exercises for 30 days to find greater peace and contentment in your life. It is said that gratitude is the highest of all human emotions, equaled only by the feeling of love.

We can be grateful any time we choose, we simply have to shift our focus to the things that we appreciate about our experience, right in that moment. Why would we choose not to feel the very highest of emotions? Why should we be content with settling for anything less?

"When you change the way you look at things, the things you look at change."
–Wayne Dyer

And yes, there is always something to be grateful for.

Recently, I was preparing to give a talk at my church about this very subject. I woke up very early the morning of the talk to prepare myself and have some calm during a usually very busy and chaotic time as we try to get six sleepy children looking their Sunday best. I got dressed, did my hair and makeup, and went through the points of my talk a few times. Feeling like, "I got this!" I went downstairs to get breakfast ready before the kids got up. The house was very dark, but we'd lived there for several weeks and I was used to navigating it without light. When I got to the bottom step, I noticed that something smelled "off" in the house, but my brain was still trying to wake up, so I didn't quite place what it was.

I had taken just a few steps on the hard tile when I stepped into something squishy and wet. And then the smell hit me. I knew instantly what it was. I had just stepped into dog poop. Our dog had gotten sick in the night and had an accident, and I had just stepped in it. "Okay, okay, I've got this," I said, desperately trying to hang onto my sense of calm, but it slipped from me a little more with each step as I hobbled to the bathroom to get cleaned up.

Then I had to deal with the mess. I have a pretty weak stomach, which doesn't serve me well as either a mom or a pet owner. So, as I was cleaning it up, I started to gag, which then made my mascara start running. All the noise woke up several of my children. My son Chance came downstairs. "What's wrong, Mom?"

"Don't come any closer," I said, throwing my hand out to stop him. "Just stay on the steps."

Morgen poked her head up from behind him. "Ew! That's so gross!"

"Yes, it is." To keep them and myself occupied, I started talking. "Now, there's always something to be grateful for, right?" We'd been practicing gratitude every night as a family at the dinner table, so they knew what I was talking about. "What can we be grateful for about this?"

Chance thought a little while. "We can be grateful it happened on the tile and not the carpet."

"Yes! Yes, we can! Good, we've got one!" I cheered as I finished cleaning it up.

Morgen then added, "I'm grateful it happened to you and not to me!"

It's a simple, silly example of how different gratitude can make a situation. Before, I would have easily been upset and stressed and probably would have spent the morning snapping at the kids. Instead, we laughed it off, and it made for a really great story for my talk.

FORGIVENESS

Whoo! This is a big one. I can now see how much bitterness and resentment I had within me prior to being diagnosed with cancer. I now believe it was in part a contributor to the development of the cancer itself. Our bodies are highly receptive to our thoughts and emotions. Our brains respond by sending chemicals into our bloodstream, and our cells respond to those chemicals. When my counselor asked me where in my body I felt the pain I was experiencing from those who had hurt me deeply, I touched the center of my chest, right above my heart. Right where the cancer had grown.

My body literally responded to my negative energy, and it manifested within me as cancer. Releasing that energy through forgiveness and love greatly aided in my recovery. I have no doubt about it.

You may think that holding onto your pain and resentment is hurting the person who caused you to feel it, but it is really only hurting yourself. You will find incredible peace and freedom in forgiveness, and that should include forgiving yourself.

Release Your Limiting Beliefs

The top 10 most common limiting beliefs are:

1. I am not worthy

2. I am not good enough

3. Money is evil

4. There is not enough time

5. Fear of failure

6. Fear of success

7. I don't deserve it

8. People will laugh at me

9. It's too late to change

10. I do not forgive myself

Rate yourself on a scale of 1-10. How strongly do you feel this is true about you? If you rate higher than a 6 on any of these limiting beliefs, I would encourage you to learn how to release them. My life and success has skyrocketed as I've learned how to let go of any conscious or unconscious beliefs that may be holding me back, and I now enjoying teaching this and sharing it with others.

BUILD YOUR DREAM THROUGH SMALL, DAILY WINS

As the creators of our own reality, our life can be anything we want it to be. We can do, be, and have anything we desire.

Sometimes it is difficult to know how to get from where we are to living the life we crave, the one that calls to us from deep within our gut. But the process can be simple, fun, and effective. I focus upon small, daily wins. I know that if I can do just one small act each day that will move me closer to my dream life and what I desire, in a year, that will be 365 acts of victory!

If you want to learn more about how to build your dream and the life you crave, I invite you to accept my free workbook found on my website www. heatherchoate.com so you can start implementing these principles of success into your life today.

Life is short, so do what you love. Embrace the moment. Find your bliss. Live in gratitude.

Above all, listen to that inner voice of guidance and trust the Lord no matter what. It is a happy way to be.

There is much love for you here,

—Heather

Rescued
Through
Writing

A JOURNAL GUIDE TO WORKING THROUGH LIFE'S CHALLENGES

Welcome to my Guided Journal Workbook. Writing has truly transformed my life, emotionally, spiritually and physically. It really is therapy!!!

Sometimes it's hard to know where to start. Life can throw some wicked curveballs at us, and I know what it's like to feel like you're barely able to keep your head above water. These exercises brought me relief, clarity, and direction in moments when I needed it the most. There is something magical that happens when you get your thoughts out onto the page. It seems that there is more space in your brain. When you express your emotions through writing, you are able to release them and let them go rather than bottling them up inside of you, increasing the internal pressure and tension. You will find more to appreciate in the moment, and using your innate creativity, you will design a life that is beautiful, precious, and delicious to you.

Each section contains exercises and prompts. Each is carefully thought out to bring more clarity and peace into your life. Enjoy the workbook – I look forward to connecting with you online or in person!

Light and love,

—Heather

SLAY THE DRAGON

When I was first introduced to this exercise, I knew it would change my life. I wasn't disappointed.

There I was, stuck, frustrated, confused, and scared. I wanted great things for my life, but it seemed that no matter how hard I tried, I never got any closer. "Nothing I do is enough," I told my mastermind group one night in February. "I work so hard, but it doesn't seem to matter. I just want things to work for me, but right now, they're not."

"You need to slay the dragon," my friend, Matt told me.

"Slay the what?" I asked, half-laughing.

"The dragon."

"Okay, what does that mean?" I asked, deciding to go along with his game.

"It means there's a dragon that's risen up inside of you and now you need to slay it."

His metaphor made sense. It did feel like there was a dragon inside me. Too many bottled up emotions, just ready to burst out and set something on fire. "How do I do that?

Matt smiled, knowing he had me, and leaned forward. "What I want you to do is get out a sheet of paper, no, get out a whole stack of paper. I think you're going to need them in this case. Then write at the top: I feel _____ (whatever your emotion is) because of _____ (what you think is causing it)."

"Okay."

"Then you write out every single thing that is bothering you. For example, I feel so mad because this person said this thing to me. I hate it when they say things like that to me. Why don't they understand? I don't feel good about myself…etc. Get it *all* out," he emphasized, "don't hold a single thing back. Don't worry about punctuation, writing in complete sentences, or anything like that. Scribble if you want to. It's not supposed to look pretty. Don't stop moving your pen until you've gotten everything out."

"All right…" I said, wondering if this would really be such a good thing or not.

"When you feel like you've gotten it all out, *every single thing*, and there's nothing left inside of you," Matt explained, "then I want you to rip it up – take it outside and burn it if you have to."

I laughed, imagining what my kids and husband would think if they saw me lighting papers on fire in our driveway. "Okay…"

"The point is you're telling your subconscious mind, 'All right, I hear you. This is what is bothering us, and this is why, and now we're done with that. Thank you for the information, we're letting it go now.'"

I nodded, starting to see the value in what he was saying.

"Oh, and this is an important point," he continued, "don't write anything positive on the paper, only the bad, negative stuff. After you've destroyed the bad stuff, aka 'Slain the Dragon,' then you can go ahead and get out a clean sheet of paper and write down what you want instead."

I thanked him for sharing it with me; a light tingling sensation filled me with an eagerness to test it out for myself and a hope rose up in me that there could really be something to this. After our meeting, I put it to the test.

I sat down and wrote out everything that was bothering me. I didn't let anything hide. No baby dragons would be spared. I pulled all of it out of me, even the really dark, scary dragons hiding in the shadows deep inside of me. They were forced out of me and became ink on the page. It wasn't pretty. It was the messiest, meanest, and most awful thing I had ever written.

I was more than eager to destroy it. I never wanted to read it and didn't want anyone else to either. But I wasn't so much ashamed as I was liberated. All those bottled-up emotions finally came out. It felt like there was room inside me to think and feel again.

We all have dragons inside. I usually see people do one of two things with their dragons. They either pacify them and lull them to sleep by choosing to "numb out" rather than face their emotions. They numb themselves with food, drugs, alcohol, social media, television, video games, and any other behavior that keeps them from having to feel what's really going on inside.

Or, they breed their dragons. They're not feeling happy inside, so they get together with their friends and let all the dragons out to breed and multiply. "Did I tell you about_____ (insert awful thing). Oh, well let me tell you!"

So often when we talk about everything that's going wrong, we get all worked up about it together, but do we actually come to any solutions about it? It might make us feel better to pull out our dragons and see that our friend's is bigger than ours, or vice versa, but all we're doing is letting the dragons out to go and breed more dragons.

We need to allow ourselves to process our emotions healthfully. This exercise is a safe and effective way to do just that. You're not going to "numb out" and think that if the dragon inside is sleeping, then it's not there. And you're not going to breathe more fire and life into the dragon by complaining and raging about it to your family and friends. You're going to get it out and then destroy it.

In letting the emotions run their course, I was ready to let them go. I brought the papers outside and took a match to them, letting the words turn to ash and smoke.

I slayed the dragon.

Now, it's your turn.

Start with filling in this sentence: I feel _____ (whatever your emotion is) because of _____ (what you think is causing it).

Remember not to stop until you've gotten all of it out. (You may go through a small forest's worth of paper if you're like me.)

After you've gotten everything out, destroy it. Burn it. Drown it. Shred it. Whatever feels best to you.

Thank yourself for the information, and tell yourself you're ready to let it go now.

Now, write down what you want instead:
Rescue yourself from negative emotions by Slaying the Dragon as often
as you need to!

DESIGN THE CASTLE

Now that your brain is pleasantly "Dragon-Free," you have the room and space to more thoroughly create the life you want. I call this phase, "Design the Castle." I think there is a castle inside of all of us, a beautiful, peaceful, happy place where we would all like to be, and what we wish our "real" lives could be like. But it doesn't have to be a fairy tale. You can have that dream life. Others have done it. They've overcome tremendous odds. You can too. After all, you just SLEW A DRAGON!!! If that doesn't make you a bad-a**, I don't know what does!

But let's not get ahead of ourselves. You might be facing some serious life challenges right now. I get that. I have too. So you might not see the value in this one. Why "daydream" when you're facing a major crisis? For now, I want you to simply allow yourself to take a "mind vacation." Allow yourself some time and space to think about what you really enjoy and what you would like to enjoy in the future. What would you really like your life to look like? The following exercises are designed to get your creative juices going. You'll know you're on the right track when you write down something that makes you feel light, free, happy, and frisky inside.

You know that feeling? You felt it often as a child. That birth of a delightful new idea. That's what we want to get to now, yes, even if things aren't so good for you right now. Tap into those things that give you that feeling of bliss, and let's start to design your castle.

Write out any other thoughts or ideas that come to you.

You're Designing Your Castle!

What would you like your life to look like?

Where would you ideally like to live?

What would you see there?

How would it smell?

What would you eat?

What would you wear?

How would you feel being in this place?

What would you do in your ideal life?

_____

How would you help/contribute to others?

BE YOUR OWN CREATIVE HERO

So, now you have this castle in the sky, and yes, hopefully there are no dragons lurking around it. Now what? Life's challenges keep coming at you. You know what you want, but how do you bridge the gap from where you are now to where you want to be?

In this exercise, I want you to use creativity to work through your challenges. You get to be your own hero here.

When I was fighting cancer, I found great relief in using the experience to create something. I used the pain and fear to make something beautiful. I wrote poems, made artistic photographs depicting what we were going through, and of course, wrote stories where I infused my personal challenges into my character's experiences.

I challenge you to do the same. Creativity can be a powerful relief valve. And what you make might inspire, help, or ease someone else's struggles.

A poem or short creative essay about what I'm experiencing:

You Are Your Own Creative Hero!

What have I learned from this experience?

How might I be able to express those lessons creatively?

How could I express it visually
(art, sculpture, photography, collage)?

How could I creatively write about this
(book, poem, blog, etc.)?

LAY THE BRICKS

Create the Foundation of the Life You Want

This is the fun part. This is where we're going to take all our creative ideas, follow the design of our "castle" and start to create the life we want. Just as all buildings need a strong foundation to withstand the elements, you need a strong foundation for your life. We're going to build it from the ground up and pattern it after the design of what you most desire.

The good thing about having your life turn to shambles is that you get to start fresh. Wipe the slate clean and begin again. Take the best of what you've been through by being a creative hero, and if any of those "dragons" start to rear their heads, well, you know what to do with them. Now, we're going to lay the foundation of your ideal life, covering each of the following areas: health, finances, relationships, and spirituality.

You're Laying the Bricks!

HEALTH

Describe your ideal body. What would it look and feel like?
What kind of energy would you have?

HEALTH

What kinds of activities would you do with your ideal body?

HEALTH

What would it mean to you to have this ideal body?

FINANCES

Describe your ideal financial state:

FINANCES

*What new opportunities or experiences would
this financial state afford you?*

FINANCES

What would it mean to you to have this ideal financial state?

RELATIONSHIPS

Describe your ideal relationship:

RELATIONSHIPS

What would it mean to you to have this ideal relationship?

SPIRITUALITY

Describe your ideal spiritual state:

SPIRITUALITY

What would it mean to you to have this ideal spiritual state?

RESCUED THROUGH WRITING

Congratulations! You've used writing to help work through some of life's challenges. Practice these exercises often, and you will find it easier and easier to move toward what you want.

I hope you have found this workbook helpful. You have developed some great ideas here. If you want further help on how to take your ideas and turn them into reality, well, that's what I do best. I'd love to work with you, help identify any of the limiting beliefs that might be holding you back, and create a game-plan on how to achieve your biggest goals.

I'd love to offer you a free one-hour coaching session, right now. Simply visit www.heatherchoate.com

I wish you all the happiness, success, and abundance in the world – thank you for allowing me to be part of your journey!

Light and love, friends!

—Heather

ABOUT THE AUTHOR

Heather Choate was born in Littleton, Colorado. Most of her time is spent homeschooling her six children while trying to squeeze in spurts of writing when she can. She enjoys daydreaming of worlds and people that don't actually exist but reflect the beauty and complexity of humanity. Her novels, *Swab* and *Frayed Crossing* are #1 bestsellers, and her latest series, the *Jonas Flash Chronicles*, is warming hearts and minds across the globe. She was diagnosed with breast cancer in June 2014 while pregnant with her sixth child, spurring her to write about her incredible journey in her memoir, *Fighting for Our Lives*. Writing is her escape from diaper changes and runny noses, but motherhood is the greatest journey and joy of her life.

CPSIA information can be obtained
at www.ICGtesting.com
Printed in the USA
BVOW09s0130200817
492486BV00002B/2/P

9 781633 536296